NEW DIRECTIONS FOR EVALUATION
A Publication of the American Evaluation Association

Gary T. Henry, Georgia State University
EDITOR-IN-CHIEF

Jennifer C. Greene, Cornell University
EDITOR-IN-CHIEF

Evaluating Tax Expenditures: Tools and Techniques for Assessing Outcomes

Lois-ellin Datta
Datta Analysis

Patrick G. Grasso
The World Bank

EDITORS

Number 79, Fall 1998

JOSSEY-BASS PUBLISHERS
San Francisco

EVALUATING TAX EXPENDITURES: TOOLS AND TECHNIQUES FOR ASSESSING
OUTCOMES
Lois-ellin Datta, Patrick G. Grasso (eds.)
New Directions for Evaluation, no. 79
Jennifer C. Greene, Gary T. Henry, Editors-in-Chief

Microfilm copies of issues and articles are available in 16mm and 35mm,
as well as microfiche in 105mm, through University Microfilms Inc., 300
North Zeeb Road, Ann Arbor, Michigan 48106-1346.

New Directions for Evaluation is indexed in Contents Pages in Education,
Higher Education Abstracts, and Sociological Abstracts.

ISSN 1097-6736   ISBN 0-7879-1552-1

NEW DIRECTIONS FOR EVALUATION is part of The Jossey-Bass Education
Series and is published quarterly by Jossey-Bass Inc., Publishers, 350 Sansome Street, San Francisco, California 94104–1342.

SUBSCRIPTIONS cost $65.00 for individuals and $115.00 for institutions,
agencies, and libraries. Prices subject to change.

EDITORIAL CORRESPONDENCE should be addressed to the Editors-in-Chief,
Jennifer C. Greene, Department of Policy Analysis and Management, MVR
Hall, Cornell University, Ithaca, NY 14853-4401, or Gary T. Henry,
School of Policy Studies, Georgia State University, P.O. Box 4039, Atlanta,
GA 30302-4039.

www.josseybass.com

Editorial Policy and Procedures

New Directions for Evaluation, a quarterly sourcebook, is an official publication of the American Evaluation Association. The journal publishes empirical, methodological, and theoretical works on all aspects of evaluation. A reflective approach to evaluation is an essential strand to be woven through every volume. The editors encourage volumes that have one of three foci: (1) craft volumes that present approaches, methods, or techniques that can be applied in evaluation practice, such as the use of templates, case studies, or survey research; (2) professional issue volumes that present issues of import for the field of evaluation, such as utilization of evaluation or locus of evaluation capacity; (3) societal issue volumes that draw out the implications of intellectual, social, or cultural developments for the field of evaluation, such as the women's movement, communitarianism, or multiculturalism. A wide range of substantive domains is appropriate for New Directions for Evaluation; however, the domains must be of interest to a large audience within the field of evaluation. We encourage a diversity of perspectives and experiences within each volume, as well as creative bridges between evaluation and other sectors of our collective lives.

The editors do not consider or publish unsolicited single manuscripts. Each issue of the journal is devoted to a single topic, with contributions solicited, organized, reviewed, and edited by a guest editor. Issues may take any of several forms, such as a series of related chapters, a debate, or a long article followed by brief critical commentaries. In all cases, the proposals must follow a specific format, which can be obtained from the editor-in-chief. These proposals are sent to members of the editorial board and to relevant substantive experts for peer review. The process may result in acceptance, a recommendation to revise and resubmit, or rejection. However, the editors are committed to working constructively with potential guest editors to help them develop acceptable proposals.

Jennifer C. Greene, Editor-in-Chief
Department of Policy Analysis and Management
MVR Hall
Cornell University
Ithaca, NY 14853–4401
e-mail: jcg8@cornell.edu

Gary T. Henry, Editor-in-Chief
School of Policy Studies
Georgia State University
P.O. Box 4039
Atlanta, GA 30302–4039
e-mail: gthenry@gsu.edu

CONTENTS

EDITORS' NOTES

This volume demonstrates how evaluation tools are used to examine the effectiveness, results, and impacts of a wide array of government "programs" found in the tax code, whose total value runs about $500 billion annually (Joint Committee on Taxation, 1996). These programs are called tax expenditures. They are defined by the Office of Management and Budget (OMB) as "revenue decreases . . . due to preferential provisions of Federal tax laws, such as special exclusions, exemptions, deductions, credits, deferrals, or tax rates" (U.S. Office of Management and Budget, 1994). Unlike most direct expenditure programs, most tax expenditures are open-ended in terms of the amounts involved, they are not subject to annual competitive appropriations, they are permanently authorized, and, until recently, their effectiveness rarely has been evaluated.

Yet tax expenditures are instruments of public policy often, but not always, aimed at goals similar to those of the more familiar direct outlay or expenditure programs. In general, tax expenditures at federal, state, and local levels tend to benefit the wealthier, and direct expenditures tend to benefit the poorer.

But whereas direct expenditure programs such as Head Start, Medicaid, bilingual education, housing vouchers, the Women, Infants and Children's (WIC) feeding program, and food stamps often have had to prove their effectiveness through rigorous outcome evaluations, tax expenditures have had something of a free ride, as far as rigorous outcome evaluations go (Howard, 1993). As such, social justice and good governance both demand determination of whether the tax expenditures are yielding the benefits anticipated in the original legislation, and whether they are as good as or better than policy alternatives in direct expenditure programs (General Accounting Office, 1993, 1994).

The articles in this issue address the challenges of conducting such evaluations. Collectively, they show how evaluation techniques and publicly available data can be applied to specific tax expenditure items. The focus for this volume is on outcome evaluation, not process evaluation, descriptive studies, or tax code administration.

Our primary point is that the familiar tools of the evaluation trade can be successfully adapted to the requirements of tax expenditure results. We advance the arguments that in many ways the data collection difficulties associated with tax expenditures are not materially different from those for numerous direct spending programs, that publicly available data often are sufficient for evaluative purposes, and that even where neither of these conditions obtains it is sometimes possible to conduct sound, informative evaluations of tax expenditures.

Evaluator participation is important in such evaluations because, despite the size, scope, and durability of tax expenditures, until recently the field has been left to budget analysts and economists. Their interest generally has focused on the pre-enactment analysis of probable forgone revenues and the distributive justice (or injustice) effects of the tax breaks. Relatively little attention is given to empirical post-enactment evaluation of their effectiveness in achieving the usually lofty economic and social objectives cited in their authorizations (Aaron and Boskin, 1980; Lewis and Michael, 1990).

However, members of Congress and others are raising questions about the relative effectiveness of various approaches to social problems. Tax expenditures increasingly are being reconsidered, either in terms of the justification for retaining some of them or as substitutes for direct spending. This implies a need for program evaluators to understand and develop strategies to address the special challenges of evaluating tax expenditures.

Some Evaluation Challenges

At least five barriers to tax expenditure evaluation have presented some methodological challenges. These include difficulty in determining how much was actually invested, privacy issues, determining appropriate comparisons, measuring results, and attribution.

With regard to actual tax expenditures, information is collected annually and in vast quantities by the Internal Revenue Service. Much is stored in boxes, in original paper form, although some (such as data permitting a match between bank records and reported interest) is retrievable through computer files. New techniques for submitting entire tax returns via computer may create a remarkable data base in the future. For the present, fairly detailed information, enough for aggregate data and interrupted time series analysis, is published in the IRS Statistics of Income Report. This has permitted correlation/regression based analyses of tax expenditure results on an aggregated basis.

Tax data on individuals and corporations are generally not available, even to most government agencies. There are only limited databases on "clients" of the various tax programs. The kinds of legislated evaluation, monitoring, and reporting requirements that frequently attach to direct spending programs are far rarer for tax expenditures. Nonetheless, application of the broad evaluation tool kit, coupled with special adaptations for tax expenditure studies, have proven effective. For example, the piece on enterprise zones, reported in this volume, applies an interrupted time series approach to examine whether a package of state-level tax benefits affected employment in three cities, using publicly available census-tract employment data. But the analysis goes beyond the statistical results by identifying specific companies to whose hiring decisions employment gains could be attributed. This information is publicly available because every business falling within the geographically defined enterprise zone is eligible to participate. Officials of these companies were interviewed to determine whether they actually took account of the tax advantages in making their decisions. Combining the quantitative and qualitative results provides a far more powerful analysis than the interrupted time series alone could deliver.

With regard to privacy issues, individual tax returns are protected by law. Further, the IRS tries to use state-of-the-art methods to prevent tampering with their computer files and to block access by hackers. There are algorithms for assuring privacy of individuals while providing information needed for surveys of both organizations and individuals who have taken certain tax expenditures. This allows for more powerful controls and richer design alternatives than aggregated regressions, sophisticated as these have become through modeling and other techniques. At present, using these algorithms depends on specific Congressional requests for the evaluations and requires additional time and expense. Alternatives for the evaluator who is not carrying out a Congressional request, directly or through a contract, include reliance on tax information provided voluntarily by interest groups and surveys of eligible individuals and organizations who may be willing to cooperate with the study as was the case, for example, with the Negative Income Tax experiments of the 1970s (Rossi and Lyall, 1978).

Turning to appropriate comparisons, two features dominate the design landscape. First, in most instances federal tax expenditures become available to all eligible individuals or organizations at the same time or are phased in or out at the same rate. Second, not all taxpayers actually take the deductions and credits for which they are eligible, creating a challenge in understanding these self-selection biases. For example, in 1993 the Earned Income Tax Credit (EITC) was worth up to $2,100 to individuals who were working, had an adjusted gross income of less than $33,370, had at least one qualifying child, and met about twelve other requirements. The IRS can report how many returns included the EITC and how much was disbursed, but does not have systematic information about how many eligible individuals did not claim what could seem like "free" money.

As to appropriate measures, tax expenditures, like direct outlays, frequently are lavishly endowed in legislation with broad, diverse, and even grandiose statements of goals justifying the exclusion, credit, or deferral. As noted, Congressionally mandated evaluations of results rarely are part of such legislation. Thus identifying exactly what would be considered a fair criterion of effectiveness can require a bit of detective work, even before the evaluator grapples with developing adequate indicators and testing the availability of reliable information. Here the evaluation tool kit can be particularly useful. Many, though not all, tax expenditures have goals similar to those of direct expenditure programs, some of which have been quite thoroughly evaluated And, as the studies discussed in this issue illustrate, evaluators have become well versed over 30-plus years in knowing how to identify measurable, relevant outcomes.

Another challenge in evaluating tax expenditures is attribution. Due care must be taken to examine the interactions among tax provisions affecting the value of a given tax expenditure in a specific year and to the generalizability of the findings. Relevant variables include tax code changes from year to year, interactions between tax expenditures and the general economy, as well as what is happening in relevant direct expenditure programs. These add considerably to the problems in estimating what would have happened without the tax expenditure and to estimating the value added of the tax expenditure.

With due care, however, evaluators have applied many of the familiar evaluation tool kit designs. In some instances, for example, the Negative Income Tax studies, multisite experimental designs were possible because this was a pre-enactment test of an approach to welfare reform. Other evaluations have applied interrupted time series and others a combination of time series analyses and participant/comparison group designs.

The attention given to attribution of results by the evaluation field may be among our unique contributions to determining whether a tax expenditure is effective. For this reason, while the difficulties are recognized, attribution is strongly emphasized in this issue. As an example, a recent evaluation of the effects of alcohol fuels tax incentives, based primarily on projections from theory and analysts' opinions, was criticized as lacking attention to benefits and to attributional issues. The U.S. General Accounting Office issued a rare follow-up report defending the study's methodology (General Accounting Office, 1997a, 1997b). Alternative designs based on program evaluation methodology, examining what actually happened with due care for attribution, could have yielded more convincing information.

The Chapters in this Volume

To get us started, we first turn to work by Bruce Davie that provides the context needed to appreciate the substantive evaluations that follow. Davie presents some of the intellectually and politically difficult issues surrounding the concept of tax expenditures. He notes, for example, that tax expenditures are defined as "special" exclusions, exemptions, deductions, credits, preferential rates, or deferrals of tax liability. But what constitutes "special" has proven contentious. Having given us fair warning that identifying tax expenditure items is itself a major task (albeit one with some guidance in the specific items recognized as tax expenditures by the Joint Committee on Taxation and the Office of Management and Budget in their reports), he then lays out the major criteria against which they might be judged. This discussion is important both for assessing the substantive evaluations that follow and for helping us direct future work on tax expenditure evaluation.

We next consider six evaluations of specific tax expenditures programs in the United States and Canada. These cases demonstrate both the diversity of tax preferences and the variety of methods that have been used to evaluate them. Each case presents an interesting methodological or analytical problem.

Two of the cases involve tax expenditures intended to address those in economic need. The first, by Carolyn J. Hill, V. Joseph Hotz, and John Carl Scholz, involves a particularly unusual tax expenditure item: the Earned Income Tax Credit (EITC). What makes this credit unique is that it provides support directly to low-income workers and it is refundable. The latter characteristic makes the EITC much more like the direct spending programs than most tax expenditure items. Hill, Hotz, and Scholz focus their evaluation on three key issues: the extent to which eligible workers actually participate in the program by claiming the credit, the effects of the EITC on labor markets and its effectiveness as a work incentive, and use of the credit by ineligible persons. To address these issues, they report on a series of studies that used a multiplicity of methods, demonstrating the importance of flexibility, especially where data gaps exist.

The second case, the Low-Income Housing Tax Credit (LIHTC) offers indirect assistance to those in need through incentives for housing construction. James E. Wallace weighs the LIHTC against several criteria: its cost effectiveness, the extent to which it provides a net addition to the housing supply, and development costs for the projects. He draws data on the program from a number of analyses and studies to support his evaluation conclusions and gives a brief discussion of alternative routes to affordable housing, comparing the tax and direct expenditure sides of the budget. Wallace's focus on the relative costs of using the tax approach to address the housing issue, as opposed to a spending approach, and the efficiency implications of the analysis are particularly enlightening.

The remaining cases deal with business and investment related tax expenditure items. This reflects the fact that legislative bodies around the world frequently resort to special tax code provisions as a way of stimulating or directing investment. Many economists argue that such incentives are bad policy for two reasons. First, they may encourage inefficient investment decisions by making favored options more attractive than the market would otherwise dictate. Second, they may be ineffective in many cases: businesses or investors may become free riders who take tax benefits for doing precisely what they would have done anyway. Four cases explore these possibilities.

First, Terry Hanford examines an intriguing financial instrument, the employee stock ownership plan (ESOP). ESOPs were developed in the 1970s to give businesses a new vehicle for raising investment funds while helping to make workers stockholders in their employing companies. In addition, proponents argued that the workers, as "owners" of the company, would likely become more attentive to the health of the firm, leading to improved productivity and profitability. This promise is the focus of Hanford's study, but he also reports on the costs of the program in relation to the benefits participants derived. What is particularly interesting here is the study's quasi-experimental design. This involved an elaborate matching protocol and multiple before-and-after measures of firms with and without ESOPs to estimate ESOP effects on productivity and profitability. Another noteworthy feature is the way some of the key measures were developed to ensure comparability among quite different businesses.

While there has been little public dispute about ESOPs, perhaps due to the mellow resonance of encouraging employee ownership, there has been substantial debate since the early 1980s about enterprise zones (EZs) for urban economic development. As that discussion proceeded, the states got well ahead of the federal government in providing tax incentives for businesses to locate or expand in clearly identified areas. Scott Crosse, Patrick G. Grasso, and Monica Kelly report on a study of the effects of Maryland's program on employment in three cities across the state. Intended to inform federal legislation, and thus an instance of a prospective case study evaluation, the design is also noteworthy as an example of a best-instance case study: Maryland was selected as a "mature, proud" example whose features were as similar as possible to those of the proposed legislation. The evaluation uses an interrupted time series analysis of employment levels in the three zones and analysis of supplemental data from a survey of individual employers. One interesting feature of this study is that follow-up interviews were conducted with employers who had moved into or increased employment in the zones to determine what incentives in the Maryland program, if any, had influenced their decisions. As it turned out, those interviews were crucial to reaching sound conclusions on the program.

The use of tax incentives to affect investment, as in the case of EZs, is one of the perennial points of contention in politics and economics. Perhaps the longest-running debate has centered on the notion of a broad-based tax credit to stimulate investment. Unlike the EZ program, the investment tax credit (ITC) is not designed to affect business location, but to provide a more general stimulus for investment in plant and equipment. Thomas Karier's analysis of the ITC looks at its effects in terms of total investment spending, the composition of the investment (that is, the extent to which the credit moved investment to plant and equipment from other uses), corporate income, and the distribution of the tax savings among consumers, employees, stockholders, and other uses. Karier takes advantage of the natural experiment provided by the fact that the ITC was an on-again, off-again program for nearly 30 years. Moreover, when it was in use, the allowable credit rate (as a percentage of applicable investment) and other features changed a number of times, offering natural variation in treatment intensity. In an interesting analogy to using program theory in evaluating direct expenditures, Karier's approach is grounded in understanding the assumptions underlying the ITC and how it is supposed to work.

Sometimes, governments decide to use tax incentives to stimulate investment in particular businesses. One example is Canada's program for encouraging investment in mining and energy companies through a special form of stock allowing certain corporate tax benefits to pass through to individual investors. In our final substantive case, Gordon J. Lenjosek reports on a major study of these flow-through shares. In evaluating this program, Lenjosek applies three criteria: the relevance of the program, that is, the extent to which it realistically addresses an identified need; its effectiveness in meeting policy objectives, including raising equity and enhancing exploration and development activities; and its cost effectiveness for a range of stakeholders, including the Canadian government, investors, mining and petroleum companies, and society in general. (Interestingly, these criteria are virtually identical to those used by the World Bank to evaluate its development projects. The study uses a variety of methods, including case studies of firms and limited partnerships, and economic and financial analyses. It offers an interesting counterpoint to Karier's ITC study because of the narrower focus of the tax incentive involved in this case.

In the closing chapter, Robert Boruch presents a critical review of the cases reported in the previous sections. His review centers on two questions. First, what is the quality of the evaluative work reported in this volume? The major thrust of this section is to critique the studies, considering the questions raised and the technical quality of the work in terms of the design, measures, and data analysis. Second, what do these studies, taken as exemplars of work in the field, tell us about the feasibility of applying the evaluation tool kit to tax expenditure programs? Here Boruch steps back from the individual studies to offer insights into whether and how this kind of work should proceed.

Lois-ellin Datta
Patrick G. Grasso
Editors

References

Aaron, H. J., and Boskin, M. J. (eds.) *The Economics of Taxation.* Washington, D.C.: The Brookings Institutions, 1980.

Howard, C. "The Hidden Welfare State: Tax Expenditures and Social Policy." Unpublished dissertation, Massachusetts Institute of Technology, 1993.

Joint Committee on Taxation. *Estimates of Federal Tax Expenditures for Fiscal Years 1997–2001.* JCT-11–96. Washington, D.C.: U.S. Government Printing Office, 1996.

Lewis, G. H., and Michael, R. C. (eds.) Microsimulation Techniques for Tax and Transfer Analysis. Washington, D.C.: The Urban Press, 1990.

Rossi, P. H., and Lyall, K. "An Overview Evaluation of the NTE Experiment," in T.D. Cook et al. (eds.), *Evaluation Studies Review Annual,* vol. 3, Beverly Hills, Calif.: Sage Publications, 1978.

U.S. General Accounting Office. *Tax Policy: Low-Income Housing Tax Credit as an Alternative Development Method.* July 1993. (GAO/RCED 93–31)

U.S. General Accounting Office. Tax Policy: *Tax Expenditures Deserve More Scrutiny.* June 1994. (GAO/GGD/AIMD 94–122)

U.S. General Accounting Office. *Tax Policy: Effects of the Alcohol Fuels Tax Incentives.* March 1997a. (GAO/GGD 97–41.)

U.S. General Accounting Office. *Response to Concerns About Alcohol Fuels Report.* June 1997b. (GAO/GGD 97–145R)

U.S. Office of Management and Budget. *Budget of the United States, Appendix Two.* Washington, D.C.: Office of Management and Budget, 1994.

LOIS-ELLIN DATTA is president of Datta Analysis. Her focus is the intersect of public policy and evaluation methodology and practice.

PATRICK G. GRASSO is senior knowledge management officer in the operations evaluation department of The World Bank.

A framework for thinking about tax expenditures is presented in the form of answers to five questions: what are they, what are they used for, how big are they, who benefits from them, and who loses? Distinctions are discussed among the use of tax expenditures to fine-tune ability to pay, to influence economic behavior, to mimic the features of a direct-spending program, and for other purposes.

Tax Expenditures: The Basics

Bruce F. Davie

The Taxpayer Relief Act of 1997 (the 1997 Act) marked a resurgence of tax expenditures. Practically all of the $420 billion of tax cuts expected to result from the 1997 Act over the 1997–2007 period take the form of increased tax expenditures. (This gross tax cut is expected to be partially offset by tax increases of $145 billion, mostly in the form of additional excise taxes. See Table 1.1.) In sharp contrast, the Tax Reform Act of 1986 (the 1986 Act) offset rate reductions by eliminating and reducing tax expenditures (Neubig and Joulfaian, 1988).

The creation of new tax expenditures and the expansion of old ones by the 1997 Act provide new opportunities both for analysts to evaluate these policy instruments and for political scientists to explain the turnabout in tax policy from 1986. This paper provides a framework for thinking about tax expenditures that should assist in both tasks. The framework takes the form of answers to five basic questions.

What Are Tax Expenditures?

The simple answer comes in two flavors: legal and empirical. The simple legal answer is taken from the Congressional Budget and Impoundment Control Act of 1974. The Act defined tax expenditures as "those revenue losses attributable to provisions of the Federal tax laws which allow a special exclusion, exemption, or deduction from gross income or which provide a special credit, a preferential rate of tax or a deferral of tax liability." The empirical answer is

---

U.S. Department of the Treasury and Georgetown University. The views expressed in this article are solely those of the author and in no manner should be attributed to the Department of the Treasury.

Table 1.1. Revenue Provisions of the Taxpayer Relief and Balanced Budget Acts of 1997
(Billions of Dollars)

| | Revenue Effects | | | | | | | | |
| | 1997–2002 | | | 2003–2007 | | | 1997–2007 | | |
	Increases	*Decreases*	*Net*	*Increases*	*Decreases*	*Net*	*Increases*	*Decreases*	*Net*
Entities affected and major items									
Individuals									
A. Income taxes									
1. Child credits	0.0	85.0	−85.0	0.0	98.3	−98.3	0.0	183.4	−183.4
2. Tuition credits	0.0	31.6	−31.6	0.0	44.5	−44.5	0.0	76.0	−76.0
3. Individual retirement arrangements	0.1	1.9	−1.8	0.0	18.4	−18.4	0.1	20.3	−20.2
4. Capital gains provisions	7.8	7.7	0.1	0.0	21.3	−21.3	7.8	29.0	−21.2
5. Home office expense	0.0	0.9	−0.9	0.0	1.5	−1.5	0.0	2.4	−2.4
6. Health insurance for self-employed	0.0	0.4	−0.4	0.0	3.1	−3.1	0.0	3.5	−3.5
7. Other, including pension provisions	12.9	16.4	−3.6	3.3	17.8	−14.4	16.2	34.2	−18.0
Total	20.7	143.9	−123.1	3.3	204.8	−201.5	24.1	348.7	−324.6
B. Estate and gift tax	0.0	6.4	−6.4	0.0	28.1	−28.1	0.0	34.5	−34.5
C. Employment taxes	6.4	0.0	6.4	0.7	0.3	0.4	7.0	0.3	6.7
Total	27.1	150.2	−123.1	4.0	233.2	−229.2	31.1	383.5	−352.4

Table 1.1. (Continued)

	1997–2002			Revenue Effects 2003–2007			1997–2007		
	Increases	Decreases	Net	Increases	Decreases	Net	Increases	Decreases	Net
Corporations and other businesses									
A. Income taxes									
1. Alternative minimum tax	0.0	8.2	-8.2	0.1	11.8	-11.7	0.1	20.0	-20.0
2. Research credit	0.0	2.2	-2.2	0.0	0.0	-0.0	0.0	2.3	-2.3
3. Amtrak NOL provision	0.0	2.3	-2.3	0.0	0.0	0.0	0.0	2.3	-2.3
4. Other	5.5	4.0	1.5	5.6	3.7	1.9	11.1	7.7	3.4
Total	5.5	16.8	-11.3	5.7	15.6	-9.9	11.2	32.4	-21.2
B. Excise taxes									
1. Airport and Airway Trust Fund taxes	34.5	1.3	33.2	46.7	0.2	46.5	81.2	1.5	79.7
2. Tobacco taxes	5.2	0.0	5.2	11.5	0.0	11.5	16.7	0.0	16.7
3. Other	1.5	0.2	1.3	1.6	0.2	1.4	3.1	0.5	2.7
Total	41.2	1.6	39.6	59.8	0.4	59.4	101.0	2.0	99.0
C. Tariffs and duties	0.0	0.4	-0.4	0.0	0.0	0.0	0.0	0.4	-0.4
Total	46.7	18.7	28.0	65.5	16.0	49.5	112.2	34.7	77.5
State and local governments	0.0	0.3	-0.3	0.0	0.5	-0.5	0.0	0.8	-0.8
Charities—501(c)(3) organizations	0.5	0.3	0.2	0.8	0.6	0.2	1.3	1.0	0.3
Total	74.3	169.6	-95.3	70.3	250.4	-180.1	144.6	420.0	-275.4

Details may not add to totals because of rounding.

Source: U.S. Congress, Joint Committee on Taxation, JCX-39-97, July 30, 1997

found annually in the *Analytical Perspectives* volume of the President's budget documents and a pamphlet published by the Joint Committee on Taxation (JCT). (See U.S. Office of Management and Budget, 1997, and Joint Committee on Taxation, 1996b, for examples.) These two sources list, with minor differences, the items identified by the Treasury and JCT staffs as meeting the legal definition and provide estimates of the revenue losses associated with each item. (Brief explanations of the listed provisions are found in Senate Budget Committee, 1996. This volume also contains references to the literature related to individual items.) Neither list attempts to be comprehensive. Estimated revenue losses have to round up to $100 million over five years to make the JCT list and exceed $5 million in a year to be listed by the Treasury. Because nothing in federal budget procedures is automatically affected by the list of items or the estimates (for reasons explained later in the chapter), the vagueness of the definition's use of the term "special" has never been a matter of great practical import.

Note that the statutory definition of tax expenditures is limited to the income tax context; the discussion in this paper is similarly constrained. The tax expenditure concept, however, can usefully be extended to other forms of taxation, including state and local government taxes. The Treasury Department annually provides estimates of tax expenditures associated with gift and estate taxes (U.S. Office of Management and Budget, 1997). For discussion of federal tax expenditures in the excise tax and payroll tax contexts, see Davie (1994) and Forman (1993).

The more complicated answer begins with the legislative history of the 1974 Act interpreting "special" to mean deviations from the "normal" structure of the income tax, and the normal structure to include personal exemptions, standard deductions, and graduated individual rates (Surrey and McDaniel, 1985; Forman, 1986). The great gray area in the definition stems from tax accounting rules in the Internal Revenue Code and provisions related to administrative convenience. Are such rules and provisions that operate to the taxpayer's advantage tax expenditures? In practice, the tradition has been to accept tax accounting and administrative rules, whatever they are, as part of the normal tax system and identify as tax expenditures only deviations from the general rules. (Beginning in 1982, the Treasury Department, which compiles the list and makes the estimates for the President's budget documents, has argued that accelerated depreciation, graduated corporate rates, and certain other features of the Code should not be treated as tax expenditures because of their general applicability. Nonetheless, the Treasury Department provides estimates of these provisions because they were part of the initial lists published pursuant to the Budget Act of 1974.) One example of the significance of this point comes from the 1986 Act and another from the 1997 Act.

The 1986 Act was developed under a revenue neutrality constraint. Revenue gains from base broadening were used to offset rate cuts and other reductions, but aggregate revenue over a five–year horizon was intended to be kept at baseline estimates. Several of the major revenue-raising provisions, widely referred to as "loophole-closers," did not involve provisions previously identified as tax expenditures. For example, the prior law "completed contract" rule allowed deferral of income recognition until long-term construction contracts were completed. The Act generally required income to be recognized as progress payments were made. Deferral under the old rules had not been listed as a tax expenditure. Following the 1986 Act, a new item appeared on the tax expenditure lists: an exception allowing continued use of the old rules for contracts involving construction of housing and certain other real estate.

The 1997 Act liberalizes the rules regarding deductions for home office expenses. Under normal income tax rules the expenses associated with earning income are deductible. Defining allowable expenses in the case of home offices has always been a troublesome exercise in drawing a line between legitimate expenses associated with working at home and disallowing a deduction for the guest room. Moving the definitional line a bit in favor of the taxpayer should not be regarded as a tax expenditure.

Several features of the corporate income tax have always provided conceptual difficulties with respect to defining tax expenditures. The individual and corporate income tax are treated as separate taxes, a so-called "classical" income tax structure. This basic tax structure taxes twice the part of corporate income paid out to individuals in the form of dividends. (When the Code allowed individuals to exclude the first $100 of dividend income received, that provision was listed as a tax expenditure.)

Nonetheless, forms of business organization that avoid corporate-level tax (for example, partnerships, subchapter S corporations, and cooperatives) have never been listed as tax expenditures. Similarly, the tax accounting rules regarding corporate mergers, consolidations, acquisitions, and divestitures have never been on tax expenditure lists. Several of the loophole-closers in both the 1986 and 1987 Acts, however, involved these corporate financial techniques.

The author's favorite illustration of the gray areas involved in identifying tax expenditures associated with the corporate income tax is the following: cooperatives are corporations exempt from the corporate income tax so long as 85 percent of their income comes from transactions with their members. Rural telephone companies had been challenged by the Internal Revenue Service during the 1970s regarding income from the sale of advertisements in the yellow pages of their directories. In some cases, categorizing such income received from nonmembers as "bad income" for purposes of the 85 percent test pushed coops over the line and subjected them to the corporate income tax. The co-ops argued that the directories were for the benefit of their members and that it was difficult to allocate the expenses of publishing the directories to the ads. Congress responded in the Miscellaneous Revenue Act of 1980 by adding section 501(c)(12)(B)(iii) to the Internal Revenue Code that disregards income "from the sale of display listings in a directory furnished to the members of the mutual or cooperative telephone company" for purposes of the 85 percent test. Reasonable experts could differ as to whether this item constitutes a tax expenditure. One could view all the rules identifying exempt co-ops as essentially arbitrary.

Another view is that this specific rule is a matter of administrative convenience, simplifying application of the basic 85 percent rule and hence not a tax expenditure. On the other hand, it seems like a "special" exclusion from income. But, as with hundreds of other Code provisions, its de minimis revenue consequences have allowed Treasury and JCT staffs to avoid answering that question.

The 1997 Act's big ticket item of a $500 credit for children under the age of 17 provides another good example of definitional niceties. Personal exemptions have always been accepted as part of the normal structure of the income tax and not a tax expenditure. Converting deductions for personal exemptions into credits would not create a tax expenditure either. If that is true, should the new child credit be listed as a tax expenditure? The answer is probably yes, because it is "special," applying to some dependents and not all and because of its income phase-out rule. But note how this provision fails to fit the popular view that all tax expenditures are spending programs in disguise. This observation raises the next question.

What Are Tax Expenditures Used for?

Tax expenditures address five major governance issues: fine-tuning the ability-to-pay principle of taxation, influencing economic behavior, mimicking direct spending programs, respecting American traditions, and placating special interests.

Fine-Tuning the Ability-to-Pay. That $500 child credit, with its phase-out rules for high-income taxpayers, can be viewed as shifting relative tax liabilities away from moderate-income and upper-middle class families with young children toward singles, childless couples, and very high-income families. Certainly its proponents did not advance the provision as a powerful incentive for having more children, nor is it a narrowly targeted tax provision that might otherwise have been designed as a spending program. Public tolerance of the income tax as a major source of government revenue stems from a widely shared sense that taxes ought to be based on ability to pay. But income has never been used as the sole measure of ability to pay. The child credit and several other tax expenditures, such as the deductibility of certain medical expenses, the deductibility of casualty losses, and the extra standard deduction for taxpayers 65 or over, can be thought of as attempts to fine-tune the ability-to-pay concept.

Tax expenditures implementing political judgments regarding ability to pay can be analyzed to determine their distributional effects and whether the complexity and compliance burdens they introduce are reasonable. Some may affect behavior in ways that need to be understood, but in several cases there is no reason to evaluate taxpayer responses. No one changes behavior in response to the added standard deduction for taxpayers 65 or older.

Influencing Economic Behavior. A tax system controlled by a popularly elected legislature is bound to reflect attempts to channel resources toward particular uses and direct consumer spending in special ways. At their best, these provisions can be seen as compensating for some market failure or overcoming myopia on the part of investors or consumers. For example, special tax treatment for research and development expenditures has been defended on the grounds that not enough R&D will be undertaken by private firms unable to capture all the social returns from their efforts. At their worst, such provisions induce resources to be wasted or reward activity that would have transpired without a tax break.

Influencing economic behavior through the tax system attracts advocates for several reasons. Policy concerns can be addressed without seeming to increase the scope of direct government activity. Unlike spending and credit programs, tax expenditures seldom require an administrative apparatus beyond what the Internal Revenue Service provides. This point can be exaggerated, however, because some tax expenditures require extensive IRS resources to administer and impose significant private compliance costs. Unlike appropriated subsidies, tax expenditures for the most part are permanent features of the law; advocates need not defend them every year.

Tax expenditures influence economic behavior by increasing the after-tax returns to particular investments or reducing the after-tax cost of consuming particular goods or services. As investors react to these provisions by expanding investment in the favored activity, economists expect the after-tax returns to the favored activity to become equal to the after-tax returns on other investments. Diminishing returns pervade. Similarly, consumption of particular goods favored by the tax system can be expected to increase in response to lower effective prices. The major task facing analysts studying particular provisions is to sort out their effect on rates of returns and prices and identify induced behavioral reactions.

The exclusion from taxable income of the interest paid on bonds issued by state and local governments provides an example. Interest rates on these obligations are bid down so that their tax-free returns equate to after-tax returns on similar taxable securities. State and local governments (and the myriad of private activities for which the tax code permits state and local governments to issue tax-exempt bonds) are the primary beneficiaries of the exclusion. Investors who buy these bonds only benefit if they are in a tax bracket higher than that which equates after-tax returns on taxable and tax-exempt securities. In Table 1.1, state and local governments are listed as entities affected by some minor provisions in the 1997 Act related to tax-exempt bonds.

The 1997 Act provides another example. It creates a major new tax expenditure—tax credits based on tuition payments for postsecondary education. Some of the arguments supporting the provision were couched in terms of influencing economic behavior. The credits were expected to induce more high school graduates to attend college and older workers to take courses to improve their job-related skills. Concerns were expressed that tuition credits would lead to increases in tuition charges (Gravelle and Zimmerman, 1997). But some of the supporting arguments for the credits were made on the basis of ability to pay. Middle-class taxpayers trying to send their children to college were thought to be particularly deserving of tax relief. This example indicates that the ability-to-pay and influencing-economic-behavior answers to why tax expenditures pervade the U.S. tax system are not mutually exclusive.

Spending Through the Tax System. Some tax expenditures go well beyond creating marginal increases in rates of return or modest reductions in prices. They are consciously designed to mimic the features of a direct spending program. Tax credits are the technique of choice in these cases because credits can provide a dollar-for-dollar subsidy. By contrast, exclusions from taxable income or special deductions depend on the taxpayer's marginal tax rate to deliver the subsidy. Such provisions add complexity in comparison with direct spending programs. A taxpayer has to have sufficient tax liability to use the credit. If not, some technique must be used to transfer the credit to taxpayers who can use it. Arranging the transfer adds to the transactions costs of a project and erodes the efficiency of the credit as a subsidy device.

The Low-Income Housing Tax Credit (LIHTC) is an example of a tax expenditure with most of the features of a direct spending program. This provision allows owners of certain housing units rented to low-income tenants to claim tax credits over a ten-year period that have a present value equal to 70 percent of the cost of building the units. LIHTC projects are typically syndicated by developers to a group of individual or corporate investors. The amount of these credits is limited; state housing agencies allocate annual quotas to developers whose proposed projects they approve. The agencies monitor compliance with detailed tax code rules (U.S. General Accounting Office, 1997). The LIHTC was added by the 1986 Act to replace other tax expenditures, primarily accelerated depreciation, that encouraged investment in low-income housing. A program making grants to state housing agencies for low-income housing subsidies could have been designed with the same features as the LIHTC and could have avoided the costs associated with "selling" the tax credits to investors willing to "buy" a stream of future tax credits. The direct approach was not taken in 1986 because it would have been outside the jurisdiction of the tax-writing committees, requiring approvals from both the authorizing committees and the appropriations committees of the House and Senate.

The 1997 Act contains a classic example of a tax credit provision designed to mimic a direct spending program. The new provision allows financial institutions to receive an annual tax credit after making a zero-interest loan to certain public schools located in poverty neighborhoods. Economically, the annual credit, which has to be taken into taxable income by the lender, is the equivalent of a taxable interest payment. In effect, the federal government pays the interest. Similar to the LIHTC, the volume of the loans that can be made, and hence the tax credits received, are fixed. State education agencies allocate the available credits to applicant schools. Clearly, financial institutions would not make interest-free loans without the tax credits. This provision is intended to channel economic activity in a new direction, not simply influence existing behavior.

The Earned Income Tax Credit (EITC), first enacted in 1976, fuzzes the distinction between the tax system and direct spending because credits in excess of tax liabilities are refunded. For 1996, the EITC was estimated to result in a revenue loss of $5.1 billion but refunds in excess of tax liabilities were estimated to have resulted in outlays of $19.2 billion. The appropriations committees of Congress perceived refundable tax credits as a threat to their jurisdictional authority over spending programs. In 1978, they sponsored legislation restricting the authority of the Internal Revenue Service to pay refunds in excess of tax liabilities with respect to any tax credit enacted after 1977 (P.L. 95–355).

Respecting American Traditions. Certain tax expenditures are best explained by the traditions of American polity. Deductions for contributions to charitable organizations are a case in point. Direct spending programs supporting some of these organizations are conceivable, but surely in the case of religious organizations indirect aid through a tax expenditure fits traditional attitudes toward the relationship between the state and churches better than direct spending. Traditions are so strong in this regard that exempting charitable institutions from income taxation has never been listed as a tax expenditure.

Excluding interest on the obligations of state and local governments from taxable income is another example. This provision has been in the tax code since the beginnings of the modern income tax in 1913. A direct subsidy for state and local government borrowing could be designed, but that would put the federal government in the position of deciding what activities of state and local governments were worthy of the subsidy. Allowing these governments to issue tax-exempt bonds for governmental purposes fits American traditions of intergovernmental fiscal comity.

Deductions for home mortgage interest seem so consistent with public attitudes toward home ownership as a basic part of the "American way of life" that this long-standing tax expenditure is politically sacrosanct. Encouraging home ownership through the tax system is seldom questioned even though a variety of other tax expenditures work at cross purposes by subsidizing rental housing.

Placating Special Interests. The dimmest possible view of tax expenditures is that they result from the rent-seeking activities of individual firms, industries, and small groups of individuals who successfully use the legislative process to their own, narrow advantage. Each analyst looking over a list of tax expenditures is likely to identify some that fall into this category rather than any of those suggested above. This view of tax expenditures was the rationale for including some tax expenditures within the ambit of the Line Item Veto Act of 1996 (Joint Committee on Taxation, 1996a). Congress gave the President power to veto not only appropriations for specific projects but provisions of tax bills affecting 100 or fewer taxpayers as well. As required by that Act, the JCT staff identified seventy-nine such provisions in the 1997 Act, the first time the procedure came into play. President Clinton exercised this new power by vetoing two of those provisions. It remains to be seen whether this technique for controlling tax expenditures will survive court challenges on constitutional grounds.

How Big Are Tax Expenditures?

Tax expenditures are measured by answering the following question: by how much would receipts increase if the provision did not exist and taxpayers made no changes in their behavior? In most instances the estimates can be derived from computerized models of individual and corporate taxes that take into account the basic parameters of the tax system. For example, in estimating the revenue loss associated with deductibility of charitable contributions, the effect eliminating the provision would have on shifting taxpayers from itemizing their deductions to taking the standard deduction would be taken into account. The effect of pushing some taxpayers into higher rate brackets would also be accounted for, as would any interactions with the alternative minimum tax.

But behavioral responses are not taken into account. In this respect, estimates of tax expenditures are fundamentally different from revenue estimates that answer a different question: by how much would receipts increase if the tax expenditure provision were repealed? In answering this latter question, revenue estimators on the Treasury or JCT staff would make allowances for behavioral responses. Again using the hypothetical repeal of deductions for charitable contributions as an example, estimators would consider the extent to which businesses would recharacterize some of what they currently list as charitable contributions as necessary and proper business expenses. Is a corporate payment to a public television station for sponsoring a particular program a charitable contribution deductible under a tax expenditure provision or an advertising expenditure deductible as an ordinary business expense? Under current law it might be deducted either way, but as a matter of corporate prestige could be listed on a tax return and in an annual report as a charitable contribution (in which case it would contribute to the measured revenue loss). If deductibility of charitable contributions were repealed, corporations would be expected to change their behavior and treat such payments as ordinary business expenses. The measured tax expenditure exceeds the revenue gain from repeal.

The 1997 Act liberalized the tax treatment of capital gains, in general by reducing the maximum rate on realized capital gains from 28 percent to 20 percent. This increased the measure of the tax expenditure involved, which is the difference between revenue received as a result of taxing realized gains preferentially and the hypothetical revenue if those same gains were taxed as ordinary income. But the expected effect on receipts is much different. The change in tax treatment is expected to increase revenues in the first few years following the change because the behavioral response of taxpayers is anticipated to result in higher realizations of accrued gains. As indicated in Table 1.1, all of the capital gains provisions in the 1997 Act are expected to produce revenue gains that a little more than offset expected loses during the 1997–2002 fiscal years. Thereafter, expected revenue losses become substantial as the gains from increased realizations phase out.

Another reason not to equate estimates of tax expenditures with revenue gains from repeal of a tax expenditure provision is that repeal is not a self-evident concept. Take the deduction for home mortgage interest for example. Repeal might hypothetically be "cold turkey"—no deductions of any amount for any taxpayer. Repeal also could be prospective with respect to mortgages closed after an effective date, or phased in by size of mortgage or size of interest payment. Revenue estimates for these different forms of repeal would obviously differ.

Some tax expenditures are best measured in present value terms. The relevant question is what is the revenue loss associated with this year's activity related to the item? This year's issuance of tax-exempt bonds implies revenue losses on into the future as long as the bonds are outstanding (including bonds to refund the original bonds). This year's revenue loss significantly understates the aggregate amount over time and the aggregate fails to take the time value of money into account. Hence, a present value measure of the future revenue loss associated with this year's activity is more meaningful than the revenue loss associated with the volume of tax-exempt bonds outstanding this year. Provisions such as accelerated depreciation that permit capital costs to be recovered for tax purposes more rapidly than economic depreciation occurs allow taxes to be lower in the near future but result in higher taxes in the distant future. The aggregate amount of deductions for capital cost recovery are the same and aggregate taxes are unaffected; only the timing is changed. Measuring the revenue loss associated with this year's activity will overstate the consequences of the provision. A present value measure is again more meaningful. (Present value measures of some items are routinely published in the part of the budget documents dealing with tax expenditures; see U.S. Office of Management and Budget, 1997.)

The twenty largest tax expenditure provisions are listed in Table 1.2, along with estimated revenue losses for fiscal year 1997 and fiscal years 1997 to 2002. These estimates were made prior to enactment of the 1997 Act. Estimates for two or more provisions cannot be added together meaningfully. Two deduction items considered together would have a revenue loss less than the sum of the two separate estimates because of the interaction with the standard deduction. Two exclusion items would have a greater revenue loss if considered jointly than separately because of the effect of pushing taxpayers into higher brackets. Realistically, if several major tax expenditure items did not exist, the parameters of the normal tax system would be different in some indeterminable way. Rates would be lower or standard deductions and personal exemptions would be higher. A simple aggregation of all the tax expenditures in the annual lists is virtually meaningless.

One final caution regarding measuring tax expenditures: measures of the revenue loss associated with particular items are always estimates, even for prior

Table 1.2. The Twenty Largest Tax Expenditures in Federal Income Taxes Fiscal Years 1998 and 1998–2002
(Billions of Dollars)

Tax Expenditure Item	1998	1998–2002
Exclusion of employer contributions for medical insurance premiums and medical care	75.8	435.7
Net exclusion of employer pension contributions and earnings	56.2	285.4
Deduction of mortgage interest on owner-occupied homes	52.1	284.8
Exclusion of capital gains at death	32.0	173.0
Deduction of state and local income and personal property taxes	40.0	169.0
Accelerated depreciation of equipment	29.3	176.0
Deduction of charitable contributions	22.3	123.4
Exclusion of Social Security benefits	18.5	100.3
Deduction of property taxes on owner-occupied homes	17.4	95.3
Exclusion of interest on public purpose state and local debt	15.7	77.2
Deferral of capital gains on home sales	15.3	81.2
Exclusion of interest on life insurance savings	11.9	68.0
Exclusion of interest on state and local debt for various private purposes	8.9	42.4
Net exclusion of Individual Retirement Account contributions and earnings	8.6	45.5
28% maximum rate on capital gains (other than agriculture, timber, iron ore and coal)	8.5	45.0
Earned income credit [a]	5.8	31.7
Exclusion of worker's compensation benefits	5.3	29.6
Exclusion of capital gains on home sales for persons age 55 and over	5.1	27.2
Graduated corporation income tax rate	4.9	27.2
Accelerated depreciation of buildings other than rental housing	4.7	13.2
Deduction of medical and long-term care expenses	4.3	26.5

[a]The figures in the table indicate the effect of the earned income credit on receipts. The effect on outlays (in billions of dollars) is 22.0 in 1998 and 118.8 for 1998–2002.

Note: These estimates do not reflect the effects of the Taxpayer Relief Act of 1997.

Source: Office of Management and Budget, Analytical Perspectives, Budget of the United States Government, Fiscal Year 1998, p. 79.

years. With direct spending programs, measures of actual expenditures for a particular line item can be tabulated after the fact. Not so with tax expenditures. Those estimates are always dependent on modeling sample tax return data.

Who Benefits from Tax Expenditures?

Just as public finance economists distinguish between the statutory incidence and the economic incidence of taxation, a clear distinction needs to be made between the statutory incidence of tax expenditures and the economic incidence of tax expenditures. Those who record tax expenditure provisions on their tax returns may not be the ultimate beneficiaries. If tax expenditures show up on the tax returns of corporations, benefits need to be traced through to individuals in their capacities as owners of capital, workers, or consumers. The economic truism that only people pay taxes has a corollary: only people benefit from tax expenditures. Like the shifting of taxes, the shifting of tax expenditures requires careful analysis.

Consider some examples of shifting the incidence of tax expenditures. The benefits of tax-exempt bonds pass through largely to the users of the bond proceeds (who may or may not be the issuers). Some benefits are retained by taxpayers subject to higher marginal rates than the tax rate that equilibrates after-tax yields on comparable taxable securities with the tax-exempt yield. Tax-exempt bond proceeds are routinely issued to build stadiums and arenas for professional sports teams. Team owners can benefit from their reduced cost of the capital but some of the benefits could also shift on to professional athletes in a position to bargain away any above-market returns temporarily enjoyed by team owners (Zimmerman, 1996).

Taxpayers reduce their taxes when they make charitable contributions. Since deductibility reduces the price (the after-tax income foregone) of making a charitable contribution and because taxpayers will respond to the lower price by making some contributions they wouldn't otherwise, some of the benefits are shifted to charities and their clients.

Some tax expenditures get capitalized into the value of assets. Provisions associated with real estate are particularly subject to this phenomenon. If properties on the National Register of Historic Places become eligible for rehabilitation credits, then surely those properties become more valuable in the hands of their owners. Demand for existing homes is increased by the deductibility of mortgage interest and some of that effect will be capitalized into their value. Current owners may not benefit; when they bought the house they also paid a price similarly influenced by interest deductibility. The owners of property at the time such tax rules change are the ones who experience the effects of capitalization, and it can work both ways. The lowering of tax rates in 1986 reduced the value of interest deductions, especially for upper-income families. This may have been reflected in some home prices.

Because the incidence of tax expenditures is so often shifted, simply distributing amounts claimed on individual tax returns by some measure of taxpayer income, such as adjusted gross income, may not be very informative. Only a very few tax expenditures are fully retained by the individual taxpayers who are the statutory claimants. The child credit created by the 1997 Act, the extra deductions for those 65 and older and for the blind, and exclusion of Social Security benefits from the taxable income of lower-income retirees are examples.

In addition to these more obvious situations in which benefits flow from taxpayers to others, employees of entities that "administer" tax expenditure provisions also benefit: the staff of the specialized housing finance agencies that issue tax-exempt bonds to finance mortgages; the syndicators who market LIHTC projects to investors; the architectural historians who certify renovated buildings as eligible for historic rehabilitation credits; or the consultants who, after the fact, identify newly hired employees with respect to whom employers can claim wage credits. These beneficiaries are often the most active constituencies supporting tax expenditures.

Who Loses from Tax Expenditures?

In some cases losers know who they are. These are the producers of close substitutes for the goods or services indirectly subsidized by narrowly targeted tax provisions. But the big losers are taxpayers whose taxes would be reduced but for the existence of tax expenditures. A tax system applying high rates to a base narrowed by numerous tax expenditures can magnify the losses to those taxpayers due to the "excess" burdens imposed by high tax rates. These are the burdens caused by tax-induced changes in behavior and generally are proportional to the square of the tax rate (Rosen, 1992). Beneficiaries of direct spending or credit programs that might be substituted for tax expenditures are also losers. But details of a counterfactual set of normal tax provisions, tax rates, and spending programs cannot be specified. So in general, no one knows whether they, individually, are losers from particular tax expenditure provisions and, if so, the extent of their losses.

Conclusions

The late Stanley Surrey coined the term *tax expenditures* during his tenure as Assistant Secretary for Tax Policy in the U.S. Treasury Department. He firmly believed that identification and analysis of tax expenditure provisions would be effective "pathways to tax reform" (Surrey, 1973). As suggested above, ambiguities in the definition of tax expenditures, difficulties in their measurement, and problems in identifying winners and losers have put obstacles in the path Surrey envisioned. The 1986 Act's base-broadening, rate-reducing reform seems an aberration in view of the extensive expansion of tax expenditures enacted in 1997.

Better and more extensive evaluation of tax expenditures, firmly grounded in the basics, could set the stage for another round of Surrey-like reform. Taxpayers may be in the mood for simplifications that would broaden the base and reduce the rates of the income tax once they experience all the complexities of the 1997 Act. Marching orders ought to be taken from St. Paul, "Leave no loophole for the Devil" (Ephesians 4:27, as translated in *The New English Bible*).

References

Davie, B. F. "Tax Expenditures in the Federal Excise Tax System." *National Tax Journal,* 1994, 47 (1), 39–62.

Forman, J. B. "Origins of the Tax Expenditure Budget." *Tax Notes*, Feb. 10, 1986, 537–545.

Forman, J. B.. "Would a Social Security Tax Expenditure Budget Make Sense?" *Public Budgeting and Financial Management*, 1993, 5, 311–335.

Gravelle, J., and Zimmerman, D. *Tax Subsidies for Higher Education: An Analysis of the Administration's Proposal.* Congressional Research Service, The Library of Congress. May 30, 1997. (97–581 E)

Joint Committee on Taxation. *Draft Analysis of Issues and Procedures for Implementation of Provisions Contained in the Line Item Veto Act (Public Law 104–130) Relating to Limited Tax Benefits.* Nov. 12, 1996a. (JCX-48–96)

Joint Committee on Taxation. *Estimates of Federal Tax Expenditures for Fiscal Years 1997–2001.* Nov. 26, 1996b. (JCS-11–96)

Neubig, T. S., and Joulfaian, D. *The Tax Expenditure Budget Before and After the Tax Reform Act of 1986.* OTA Paper 60, Office of Tax Analysis, U.S. Treasury Department, October 1988.

Rosen, H. S. *Public Finance.* (3rd. ed.) Homewood, Ill.: Irwin, 1992.

Senate Budget Committee. *Tax Expenditures: Compendium of Background Material on Individual Provisions.* Dec. 1996. (S. Prt. 104–69)

Surrey, S. S. *Pathways to Tax Reform.* Cambridge, Mass.: Harvard University Press, 1973.

Surrey, S. S., and McDaniel, P. R. *Tax Expenditures.* Cambridge, Mass.: Harvard University Press, 1985.

U.S. General Accounting Office. *Tax Credits: Opportunities to Improve Oversight of the Low-Income Housing Program.* Mar. 1997. (GAO/GGD/RCED-97-55)

U.S. Office of Management and Budget. "Special Analysis G. Tax Expenditures." *Special Analyses, Budget of the United States Government, 1983.* Feb. 1982.

U.S. Office of Management and Budget. "Tax Expenditures." *Analytical Perspectives, Budget of the United States Government, 1998.* 1997.

Zimmerman, D. *Tax-Exempt Bonds and the Economics of Professional Sports Stadiums.* Congressional Research Service, Library of Congress. May 29, 1996. (96–460 E)

BRUCE F. DAVIE *is a financial economist at the Office of Tax Analysis, U.S. Department of the Treasury, and professorial lecturer at the department of economics, Georgetown University.*

The Earned Income Tax Credit is expected to cost the federal government $27.1 billion in 1998, making it the largest cash or near-cash program available to low-income families in the United States. Strategies most commonly employed to gain insight into the central issues of this tax credit include data sleuthing, simulations, natural experiments comparing participant and control groups, and cross-sectional econometric techniques.

Evaluating Work-Related Cash Benefit Programs: The Earned Income Tax Credit

Carolyn J. Hill, V. Joseph Hotz, John Karl Scholz

The Earned Income Tax Credit (EITC) was enacted in 1975 as a credit on the federal income tax, targeted primarily to working poor families with children. Major tax reforms in 1986, 1990, and 1993 have increased the amount of the credit and adjusted requirements for eligibility. In 1998, 18.3 million families are projected to receive the EITC at a cost to the federal government of $27.1 billion (Committee on Ways and Means, 1996, p. 809). As a way of providing support for low-income households through the tax system instead of through the transfer system, the EITC is often described as a program that "makes work pay" and is an important component of recent welfare reform efforts. Debate continues, however, over optimal design and targeting of the credit. Concerns focus on three primary issues. First, do those who are eligible for the credit actually receive it? Second, does the EITC, in fact, "make work pay," or are there detrimental labor market effects? Finally, to what degree do persons who are ineligible for the credit receive it? Many analyses of these issues rely on publicly available data such as the Current Population Survey or the Survey of Income and Program Participation. Recent study design features include the use of instrumental variables, which may lead to more accurate estimates of the credit's labor supply effects.

The views expressed in this paper are those of the authors and do not necessarily represent those of the U.S. Department of the Treasury.

What is the Earned Income Tax Credit?

The EITC is a credit that taxpayers receive by filling out a federal tax form and meeting certain eligibility criteria. Unlike most credits and deductions in the federal individual income tax system, the EITC is refundable. Thus, if the amount of credit exceeds the household's tax liability, the household receives a payment from the U.S. Treasury for the difference. Taxpayers eligible for the EITC may receive the credit in advance payments with their paychecks during the year. However, fewer than one percent of EITC recipients take advantage of this option (U.S. General Accounting Office, 1992, p. 10).

The EITC was promoted initially as an offset of the Social Security payroll tax for low-income working parents. Since introduction of the credit in 1975, policymakers have justified expansions of the EITC as payroll taxes have increased, the purchasing power of the minimum wage has eroded, and mechanisms outside the transfer system have been sought to supplement incomes of low-wage working parents. Bipartisan support has bolstered the EITC as a mechanism for addressing these concerns. Understanding the structure of the EITC and its growth over time are helpful for developing evaluation strategies for various aspects of the credit.

Structure of the Credit. A family's EITC is determined both by the number of qualifying children in the household and by the household's earnings from work. Beginning in 1994, filers without qualifying children became eligible for a small credit ($332 maximum in 1997), though the bulk of EITC benefits go to low-income households with children: in tax year 1994, 21.4 percent of EITC claimants did not claim a qualifying child, but received less than 5 percent of total EITC benefits (U.S. Internal Revenue Service, 1997).

Qualifying Children. To claim a child for EITC purposes, a taxpayer must show that the child satisfies age, residency, and relationship requirements. In particular, a qualifying child for the EITC must be age eighteen or younger throughout the year (persons under age twenty-four who are full-time students or persons any age who are permanently and totally disabled may be qualifying children if they satisfy the following two requirements); be the child, stepchild, adopted child, grandchild, or foster child of the taxpayer; and reside with the adult filer for more than half the year (a foster child must live with the filer for the entire year).

These requirements differ from the criteria under which a taxpayer may claim a child for a dependency exemption; generally, a filer may claim a child as a dependent only if he or she provides over half of the child's support. Furthermore, the criteria for a qualifying child for EITC purposes differ from those under which a taxpayer may claim the recently enacted child credit, instituted as part of the Taxpayer Relief Act of 1997. This $400-per-child credit is available to eligible filers beginning in tax year 1998 (the credit increases to $500 per child in subsequent years). Taxpayers may be eligible to claim this child credit for each child who is age 16 or younger throughout the year, who satisfies a relationship test, and for whom the taxpayer can claim a dependency exemption. Taxpayers must list a Social Security number or taxpayer identification number for each child they claim for a dependency exemption, for a child credit, or for EITC purposes.

Income. Along with the presence of a qualifying child, the amount of earned income (or adjusted gross income if greater) determines a household's EITC. Earned income for EITC purposes includes taxable earned income such as wages, salaries, tips, union strike benefits, long-term disability benefits, and net earnings from self-employment; and nontaxable earned income such as voluntary salary deferrals and reductions, combat zone pay, basic quarters and subsistence allowances for military personnel, and anything of value received for services performed.

Three distinct income ranges, referred to as the phase-in, flat, and phase-out ranges of the credit, are relevant to the rate and amount of credit that a taxpayer can receive (Figure 2.1). In the phase-in range, the credit amount increases as earned income increases. For taxpayers with one child in 1997, earnings of $1 to $6,500 place a household in the phase-in range, in which the credit is at a rate of 34 percent for each dollar earned up to $6,500. Taxpayers with earned income above $6,500 but below $11,930 are in the flat range of the credit and are eligible for the maximum credit of $2,210 (34 percent of $6,500). Filers with income greater than $11,930 are in the phase-out range of the credit, in which the credit is reduced by 15.98 cents for each additional dollar earned. EITC benefits are zero at incomes of $25,760 or more. Families with two or more children are entitled to a larger credit rate (40 percent of each dollar earned) up to a maximum credit of $3,656 on earnings of $9,140, after which they face a phase-out rate of 21.06 percent.

Growth of the Credit. The EITC was expanded as part of the Tax Reform Act of 1986 (TRA86), the Omnibus Budget Reconciliation Act of 1990

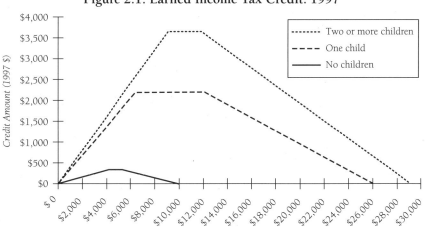

Figure 2.1. Earned Income Tax Credit: 1997

Earned Income or Adjusted Gross Income

(OBRA90) and the Omnibus Budget Reconciliation Act of 1993 (OBRA93). Table 2.1 shows major expansions of credit amounts and credit rates since the EITC was first introduced. OBRA93 enacted sharp expansions of the EITC, increasing the phase-in rate and the maximum available credit, and extending availability of the credit to childless taxpayers. The maximum credit has grown, in nominal terms, from $400 in 1975 to $3,656 in 1997 for households with two children. This growth has been driven in part by increases in the phase-in rates, from 10 percent in 1975 to 34 percent in 1997 for one-child households and to 40 percent for two-child households. Phase-out rates also have increased, albeit not to the same degree as phase-in rates.

Credit amounts were indexed for inflation beginning in 1987. The real value (in 1993 dollars) of the maximum EITC varied from $739 and $1,068 between 1975 and 1990. In 1997, the real value of the EITC is roughly three times its 1990 level as a consequence of the 1990 and 1993 changes.

What are the Primary Issues in Evaluating the EITC?

The primary administrative and policy issues of the EITC are ensuring that eligible workers receive the credit; identifying the EITC's labor market effects and structuring the credit to maximize work incentives; and minimizing receipt of the credit by ineligible individuals. Creative data sleuthing, simulations, natural experiments, and conventional cross-sectional econometric techniques are the strategies most commonly used to gain insight into these central issues. Analyses employ publicly available data as well as data acquired through special agreements with state and federal authorities. In this section, we discuss briefly each of the central issues noted above, describe studies that have addressed each issue, and highlight the studies' methodological drawbacks and strengths.

EITC Participation. The effectiveness of the EITC depends in part on whether those eligible for the credit actually receive it. The percentage of eligible households receiving the EITC—the participation rate—is reduced by eligible households that do not file tax returns, and by households that file tax returns and are eligible for the credit but do not claim it. Increasing receipt of the EITC by the former group, in particular, is a challenge for effective administration of the credit. Some families without positive tax liabilities are not legally required to file returns, yet the antipoverty effectiveness of the credit is reduced to the extent that these low-income households who qualify for the EITC do not file tax returns and receive the credit.

Estimating the participation rate of the EITC is straightforward in concept, yet difficult in practice. First, the eligible population must be estimated using information about income and presence of children. Tax returns provide information about income and dependents, but tax data are inappropriate for estimating eligibility for the EITC because some eligible households do not file tax returns. Further, family relationships, filing status, or income may be misreported on tax returns (for example, 39 percent of overclaimed amounts

Table 2.1. EITC Program Parameters, Selected Years
(dollar amounts unadjusted for inflation)

Year	Credit Rate (percent)	Flat Region		Maximum Credit	Phase-Out Region	
		Beginning Income	Ending Income		Phase-Out Rate (percent)	Ending Income
1975-78	10.00	$4,000	$4,000	$400	10.00	$8,000
1985-86	14.00	$5,000	$6,500	$550	12.22	$11,000
1987	14.00	$6,080	$6,920	$851	10.00	$15,432
1990	14.00	$6,810	$10,730	$953	10.00	$20,264
1991						
one child	16.70	$7,140	$11,250	$1,192	11.93	$21,250
two children	17.30	$7,140	$11,250	$1,235	12.36	$21,250
1993						
one child	18.50	$7,750	$12,200	$1,434	13.21	$23,050
two children	19.50	$7,750	$12,200	$1,511	13.93	$23,050
1994						
one child	26.30	$7,750	$11,000	$2,038	15.98	$23,755
two children	30.00	$8,425	$11,000	$2,528	17.68	$25,296
no child	7.65	$4,000	$5,000	$306	7.65	$9,000
1997						
one child	34.00	$6,500	$11,930	$2,210	15.98	$25,760
two children	40.00	$9,140	$11,930	$3,656	21.06	$29,290
no child	7.65	$4,340	$5,430	$332	7.65	$9,770

Source: U.S. House of Representatives Green Book, and Office of Tax Policy, U.S. Treasury Department.

among EITC claimants with children result from claiming children who do not meet the EITC residency requirements) (Scholz, 1997, p. 5). Second, data such as program administrative files or surveys contain information useful for estimating EITC eligibility, yet these sources do not contain accurate information on receipt of the credit.

Studies. Efforts to estimate the EITC participation rate link various data sources, sometimes through special agreements with state agencies, tax authorities, or other agencies, to measure EITC eligibility and recipiency. Scholz (1994), using data from the Survey of Income and Program Participation (SIPP), estimates that 9.6 to 10.3 million taxpayers were eligible for the EITC in 1990. Using this baseline estimate of eligibility Scholz derives EITC participation rates from three different data sources on EITC recipiency: the U.S. House of Representatives *Green Book,* household tax returns, and a tax topical module in the SIPP. His preferred estimates of the EITC participation rate in 1990 range from 80 to 86 percent. These rates are fairly high compared to participation rates for other types of transfer programs. For example, Blank and Ruggles (1996) estimate participation rates of 62 to 70 percent for Aid to Families with Dependent Children (AFDC), and 54 to 66 percent for the food stamps program.

A recent report by Hill, Hotz, Mullin, and Scholz (1997) estimates EITC eligibility and participation rates for a subset of potential credit beneficiaries—households receiving AFDC. The sample consists of households on AFDC during 1992 or 1993 in four California counties. AFDC households in these counties were part of the California Work Pays Demonstration Project (CWPDP), a waiver demonstration that used a randomized experimental design to assess the impact of a series of reforms to the AFDC program in the state. While the report does not explicitly exploit the underlying experimental design, it capitalizes on the data available through the demonstration project to estimate EITC eligibility and participation rates for these low-income households. Assistance unit records from county-level AFDC administrative files and quarterly earnings reports from the state's unemployment insurance (UI) system provide information about presence of children and family income. An interagency agreement between the California Department of Social Services (CDSS) and the state Employment Development Department allowed matching of AFDC administrative files to UI records. EITC participation is observed by matching the AFDC households with federal tax returns, made possible by a strict set of protocols negotiated by CDSS and the California Franchise Tax Board (FTB). Under this agreement, linking and analyses of data that involved tax returns were performed by FTB staff on FTB computers. Summary statistics from these analyses were provided to the authors of the report.

This study underscores the importance of subgroup analyses. EITC eligibility and participation rates vary across subsamples, with higher eligibility rates for two-adult households than for households headed by one adult, and higher rates for recent entrants to the AFDC system compared to households that are longer-term aid recipients. In particular, 22 to 41 percent of sample households headed by one adult, and 26 to 53 percent of sample households headed by two adults, are eligible for the EITC. EITC participation rates for these groups are 42 to 54 percent, and 61 to 84 percent, respectively (Hill, Hotz, Mullin, and Scholz, 1997). The EITC participation rates by AFDC households in this sample are lower than estimates Scholz (1994) obtained for the U.S. population, but not substantially lower, especially among two-adult households.

Some Methodological Points. The primary data sources—surveys, program administrative files, and tax returns—used to estimate EITC eligibility and participation have potentially serious limitations stemming from accuracy and coverage. First, the accuracy of the data may be affected by recall ability of respondents and, particularly in the case of administrative and tax data, by program or reporting incentives. The ability of respondents to recall precisely their household responsibilities, amount of income, or receipt of the credit may result in biased estimates of EITC eligibility and recipiency. In the case of administrative data, programs may create incentives to over- or underreport income or household responsibilities. Second, coverage of the data may be problematic. Beyond the standard concerns about selectivity of survey responses, biases may result from legal requirements and other factors affecting program enrollment or data availability for certain types of persons or groups. Concerns about accuracy and coverage should not preclude the use of surveys and administrative data, but evaluators should be aware of this potential for bias and be cautious in the interpretation of their results.

Labor Market Effects. The EITC is sometimes described as a policy that "makes work pay," but the structure of the credit suggests possible negative effects on work effort. The labor market effects of the credit can be separated into two elements: whether to work, and how much to work conditional on participating in the labor force. For persons who do not work, the credit offers an incentive to enter the labor force because the wage rate is subsidized by the phase-in rate of the EITC. For persons already in the labor force, however, work incentives differ depending on the worker's level of income. The phase-in region of the credit offers a wage supplement for each additional dollar earned. This leads to offsetting effects for work effort: the wage supplement indicates that the worker will want to work more hours, while the additional income gained indicates that the worker will want to use the money for things he or she enjoys, namely leisure, and thus will work fewer hours. The net effect of these offsetting influences is not predictable by theory. Workers with income in the flat region of the credit do not gain additional EITC benefits by working more, and can obtain the same amount of credit by working less. Thus, workers in the flat range of the credit are predicted to work fewer hours. Workers with income in the phase-out region of the credit face unambiguous incentives to reduce the number of hours they work: the marginal tax rate increases with each additional dollar earned, due to the EITC phase-out rate, thus leading workers to work less and consume more leisure. Economists refer to the wage changes associated with the EITC phase-in range as offsetting income and substitution effects, with the flat range as a pure income effect, and with the phase-out range as income and substitution effects in the same direction (discouraging work).

Attempts to evaluate actual labor market effects of the EITC encounter three main complications. First, workers who are eligible for the EITC face marginal tax rates that likely are affected by a number of other taxes and transfers. These include the payroll tax, state taxes, other federal taxes, and the benefit reduction rates associated with Supplemental Security Income (SSI), AFDC, food stamps, and other transfer benefits. Carefully modeling these interactions is crucial for isolating the effects of the EITC, because direct experimental tests are seldom possible. The second complication is linked to the first: a person's labor supply decision affects the marginal tax rate that he or she faces, and vice versa. This endogeneity creates difficulties for untangling causal effects. Third, awareness of the credit, and the degree to which labor market behaviors change as a direct response to the credit, are difficult to ascertain. As noted previously, almost all EITC recipients receive the credit as a lump sum payment. Thus, even though EITC benefits may become more or less generous, a tax filer may not become aware of these changes until she files a tax return. Eligible nonfilers may never become aware of the credit. Furthermore, many EITC recipients use tax preparers and may not realize that their tax liability is decreased by the EITC. Efforts to evaluate the credit's labor market effects have addressed these complications to varying degrees. Early studies focused on changes in hours worked, while more recent studies have addressed both hours worked and labor force participation.

Studies on Hours Worked. Studies by Hoffman and Seidman (1990), and the U.S. General Accounting Office (1993) simulate responses to the EITC by estimating the number of workers in each credit range of the EITC, then estimating responses to changes in marginal tax rates derived from the early 1970s Seattle/Denver Income Maintenance Experiment (SIME/DIME). Hoffman and Seidman use data from the Panel Study of Income Dynamics and estimate that in 1988, hours worked increased for workers in the phase-in range of the credit, while hours decreased for those in the flat and phase-out ranges. Over all groups and all ranges of the credit, total hours worked dropped by 2 percent, or about thirty-one hours a year (1990, p. 45). The GAO study examines hours effects of the EITC in 1988 and 1994 using households in the March 1989 Current Population Survey (CPS). Simulating hours effects of the EITC using response estimates derived from the SIME/DIME, the GAO estimated that hours worked decreased by 1 to 3 percent in 1988 (twenty-four to thirty-four hours a year) and by 1.5 to 5 percent in 1994 (forty-three to sixty-two hours per year) (U.S. General Accounting Office, 1993). (The GAO used OBRA90 parameters to simulate the 1994 effects, though the EITC parameters for 1994 were changed subsequently through OBRA93. The earlier parameters were used because the simulations were completed before the OBRA93 parameters were available.)

One drawback of these early studies is the use of the SIME/DIME response estimates, which may not be accurate predictors of labor responses to the EITC (we consider this issue in the methods discussion as the end of this section). A second drawback is the omission of the credit's effect on labor force participation. More recent studies on the EITC's labor market effects address both these issues.

Studies on Labor Force Participation and Hours Worked. Three recent studies (Dickert, Houser, and Scholz, 1995; Eissa and Liebman, 1996; Eissa and Hoynes, 1997) evaluate the EITC's effects on both labor force participation and hours worked for different groups of EITC-eligible households.

Dickert, Houser, and Scholz (1995) identify labor market effects from the 1993 EITC expansions for single-parent families, primary earners in married couples, and secondary earners in married couples. Using data from the 1990 SIPP, they simulated the expected effects on labor market participation and hours worked. The simulation modules allow for interactions among AFDC, food stamps, SSI, federal and state income taxes, and payroll taxes to accurately model the marginal tax rate faced by a household.

The study estimated a bivariate probit equation to predict labor force participation and, incorporating these estimates into the simulation model, found that once the 1993 expansions were fully phased in, labor force participation was expected to rise by 3.3 percentage points for single parents, to rise by .7 percentage point for primary earners in two-parent families, and to decrease for secondary earners in two-parent families. Dickert, Houser, and Scholz found that while the EITC increased hours of work for individuals in the phase-in range, the credit reduced hours of work for those in the flat and phase-out ranges. When aggregated, EITC recipients were estimated to reduce hours of work by an average of eleven hours per year (p.41). Furthermore, the findings on hours of work and labor market participation taken together imply that the increase in labor force participation more than offsets the reductions in hours worked by persons already in the labor force (p. 41).

In an interesting approach to the problem of attribution, Eissa and Liebman (1996) compare the labor force participation and hours worked of single women with children before and after TRA86. The study uses data from the March CPS in 1985–87 and 1989–91, covering tax years 1984–86 and 1988–90. To control for unobserved changes in the economy as well as other TRA86 changes that might affect behavior, Eissa and Liebman used a difference-in-differences approach, with multiple treatment and control groups, to identify the labor market effects of the EITC expansion (see Meyer, 1995, for a discussion of the difference-in-differences estimation method). Accurate estimates can be obtained from the difference-in-differences approach only if two assumptions hold: that contemporaneous shocks do not have differential effects on the treatment and control groups; and that no underlying trends, unobserved by the evaluator, affect the outcome of interest for either group.

The primary treatment and control groups employed by Eissa and Liebman for the difference-in-differences method were, respectively, single women with children and single women without children (these groups include women at all income levels). The difference-in-differences estimation showed an increase in the labor force participation rate by the primary treatment group of 2.4 percentage points, from 72.9 to 75.3 percent.

Eissa and Liebman used additional treatment and control groups to examine the robustness of their findings from the primary groups. Alternative treatment groups were single women with children and low levels of education (with separate estimates for women with fewer than twelve years of education and those with exactly twelve years), and single women with children who are predicted, on the basis of factors such as age, race, state, and education level, to have earned income in the EITC-eligible range. Alternative control groups were single women without children and with low levels of education, and single women with children and greater than 12 years of education. Difference-in-difference estimation results using these alternative groups showed labor force participation rate increases ranging from 0.9 to 4.1 percentage points.

A comparison of the treatment and control group characteristics, however, showed systematic differences between the groups. For example, members in the treatment group tended to be older, less educated, and less likely to have participated recently in the labor force. To control for these differences, Eissa and Liebman estimated a regression equation including an interaction term intended to capture the effect of the EITC on the treatment group relative to the control group, holding other observable factors constant. They found that the TRA86 expansion increased the labor force participation rate of all single women with children by up to 2.8 percentage points, from 73 to 75.8 percent. They found no change in hours worked across various subsamples of single women with children.

Eissa and Liebman explored alternative explanations for these effects, including different long-run trends in labor force participation for women with and without children, changes in the economic environment that may have affected the two groups in different ways, or unobserved shocks correlated with the demographic characteristics of either group. They reported, however, that these alternatives did not explain the relative increase of labor force participation of single women with children following TRA86. Furthermore, they presented evidence on the timing of the post-1987 participation increase, the return from the first child in a tax filing unit, and the large effect of the EITC on people most likely eligible for the credit. These factors, Eissa and Liebman pointed out, increased the likelihood that the effect is attributable to the EITC, not to other elements of TRA86.

Labor market effects for married couples with children were estimated by Eissa and Hoynes (1997). With a sample of married couples ages twenty-six to fifty-four from the 1985 to 1996 March CPS (for tax years 1984 to 1995), they used difference-in-differences to estimate labor force participation and hours effects of EITC expansions, and used instrumental variable techniques to estimate changes in hours for married men and women who are in the labor force. The difference-in-differences approach was similar to that used by Eissa and Liebman (1996), with the primary treatment group in the Eissa and Hoynes study of married couples with children, and the primary control group of married couples without children. Alternative treatment groups included subsamples of married couples with children by level of the wife's education (less than, equal to, and greater than twelve years of education). Alternative control groups were the corresponding subsamples of married couples without children. Key assumptions regarding contemporaneous shocks and underlying trends that are necessary to use the difference-in-differences approach were the same as described for Eissa and Liebman (1996). Difference-in-differences regression results showed that the EITC expansions have offsetting effects of labor force participation and hours worked for married men, but reductions in both labor force participation and hours worked for married women. The effects were not large, however. For married men, the OBRA93 EITC expansions resulted in changes in labor force participation rates of between –0.03 to 0.5 percentage point, depending on the subsample examined. The participation response appears to counteract any negative hours of work response, with findings that total hours of work increase by nineteen to fifty-one hours. For married women, those with twelve or more years of education were predicted to increase labor force participation by 1.2 to 2.5 percentage points, but women with fewer than twelve years of education were predicted to decrease labor force participation by .9 percentage point.

Due in part to the difficulty of finding a suitable control group for the difference-in-differences method, Eissa and Hoynes turned to an instrumental variable (IV) approach to examine the labor market effects of the credit. Obtaining accurate estimates with an IV approach requires choice of a variable for the regression estimates that is independent of the outcome variable (that is, hours worked) but correlated with the "treatment" variable (that is, the expansion of the EITC). Eissa and Hoynes developed two sets of IV equations. The first used the EITC tax parameters, cohort and education dummies, interactions among these variables, and a variable to indicate the first point at which income may be affected by transfer reductions or taxes (other than the EITC). The second IV equation used imputed marginal tax rates, based on $5,000 increments of income, that take into account AFDC and food stamp benefits, payroll taxes, the EITC, and other federal and state income taxes. These instrument sets varied both cross-sectionally and over time. The IV equations produce estimates of wage and income elasticities, or the percentage change in hours worked given a percentage change in wage rate or income. Eissa and Hoynes used these elasticity estimates to simulate effects of the 1993 EITC expansions on hours worked by married men and women already in the labor force. Using estimates of labor supply responses from the IV methods, Eissa and Hoynes noted that hours of work by married men and women in the phase-in region of the credit increased 1.2 to 6.6 percent and 4.3 to 16.8 percent, respectively. They found relatively large reductions in hours of work— from .4 to 18 percent—for men and women (the larger effects for women) in the flat and phase-out regions, indicating that the net effect on hours worked is negative and significant. Unlike the difference-in-differences estimates, the simulations using IV estimates did not account for additional hours of new entrants into the labor market.

Some Methodological Points. Several studies of the EITC's labor market effects have used labor response estimates derived from SIME/DIME, but these response estimates may not be applicable to EITC effects for two main reasons. First, responses to the EITC are being estimated almost twenty years after the SIME/DIME. Changes in labor responses over time or changes in the composition of the low-income population could mean that the SIME/DIME estimates are no longer accurate predictors of labor response. Second, participants in the SIME/DIME may have been more aware of the link between their work effort and after-tax income than workers today are aware of the EITC's effects on their marginal tax rates. Thus, using the SIME/DIME response parameters to estimate labor market effects of the EITC likely results in estimates that are upwardly biased, showing a greater change in hours worked in response to changes in marginal tax rates than may actually occur.

Major contributions of recent studies include modeling the impact of other taxes and transfers on marginal tax rates for low-income households, and the inclusion of labor force participation effects. As the studies by Dickert, Houser, and Scholz (1995), Eissa and Liebman (1996), and Eissa and Hoynes (1997) show, increased labor force participation has important offsetting effects for reductions in hours of work by low-income households in the credit's flat and phase-out regions.

The methods used in recent studies have certain drawbacks, however. First, simulations show expected labor market effects of the EITC, not actual effects. To the extent that labor response estimates used in the simulations are biased, or to the extent that awareness of the credit is low and persons cannot respond to the EITC because they don't know about it, the results of the simulations are also biased. Second, estimates of labor market effects obtained from difference-in-differences approaches are problematic due to the difficulty in finding appropriate control groups. Despite efforts to control for observable differences between the treatment and control groups, it is not clear that the identifying assumptions hold (that is, no contemporaneous shocks that differentially affect the treatment and control groups, and no underlying trends in either group that affect the outcome of interest). Likewise, it is not clear that the composition of the treatment and control groups is stable over time. Furthermore, it is likely that those families with children in the treatment groups in studies by Eissa and Liebman (1996) and Eissa and Hoynes (1997) face greater hurdles to entering the labor force, or even to changing hours of work, than do members of the control groups who do not have children. Finally, difference-in-differences estimators are directly applicable only to continuous outcome variables, not to discrete outcomes such as labor force participation. Given these concerns, estimates of the EITC's labor market effects from the difference-in-differences approach should be interpreted with caution.

The IV methods used by Eissa and Hoynes (1997) offer a promising set of approaches for identifying the EITC's labor market effects. These techniques overcome some of the problems noted above with dated labor response estimates and with simulations that use these response parameters. Effects of labor force participation are important to include in future models, and further work on appropriate instrument sets is in order. These structural models hold promise for more accurately estimating labor supply effects of the EITC. Another approach pursued in a study in progress by Hill, Hotz, Mullin, and Scholz uses the increasing divergence of credit amounts for families with one child relative to those with two or more children in an empirical examination of the EITC's effects on labor force participation and hours worked for a sample of low-income households.

Compliance. The third major challenge for effective design of the EITC is receipt of the credit by ineligible claimants. Such noncompliance may be inadvertent or purposeful, occurring as a result of negligence, mistakes, confusion, or fraud. An IRS study of EITC claims in tax year 1994 found that $4.4 billion, or 25.8 percent of total EITC claims, exceeded the amount for which taxpayers were eligible. With some of the mathematical error procedures now in place, the overclaim rate would have been 20.7 percent, or $3.6 billion in 1994 (U.S. Internal Revenue Service, 1997). The three most common reasons for overclaims among EITC claimants with children are: (1) claims of children who do not meet the residency requirement for EITC purposes (accounting for 39 percent of overclaimed amounts); (2) misreports of filing status (31 percent of overclaims); (3) and complex household structures in which ineligible caregivers claim a child for EITC purposes (18 percent of overclaims) (Scholz, 1997, pp. 5–6). Note that overclaims may stem from more than one of these factors. Among EITC filers who do not claim children, most errors arise from misreporting income, though 40 percent of overclaimed amounts for this group are traced to misreported filing status (Scholz, 1997, p. 6).The Taxpayer Relief Act of 1997 includes the following provisions (effective beginning in tax year 1997) that target EITC noncompliance: the act (1) denies EITC eligibility for ten years to a taxpayer who fraudulently claims the EITC; (2) denies EITC eligibility for two years to a taxpayer who claims the EITC due to reckless or intentional disregard of rules; (3) classifies a taxpayer who has been denied the EITC as a result of deficiency procedures as ineligible to claim the credit in subsequent years unless the taxpayer provides evidence of eligibility for the credit; and (4) imposes "due diligence requirements" on paid tax preparers who prepare EITC claims for taxpayers.

Studies. Examination of EITC noncompliance by researchers outside the IRS has focused primarily on characteristics of ineligible claimants, using data such as the IRS's Taxpayer Compliance Measurement Program (TCMP) studies, surveys, and administrative data.

Liebman (1995a) took advantage of the TRA86 EITC changes and reasoned that noncompliance due to inadvertent errors should not increase following the tax law changes, while fraudulent behavior would be expected to respond to the increased benefits. Using cross-sectional data from the 1985 and 1988 Taxpayer Compliance Measurement Program (TCMP) studies, he estimated the probability that a taxpayer claims excess dependent children in response to incentives by the EITC (claiming excess children is now much more difficult because taxpayers must provide a valid Social Security numbers for each child). Additionally, the study employed a difference-in-differences approach to examine responses by households with incomes above and below the maximum income eligible for EITC benefits. Liebman's findings indicated that low-income households without children are more likely to claim a dependent child than are higher-income households, and that the probability of these claims by low-income households increased relative to higher-income taxpayers following the TRA86 EITC expansions. Furthermore, he inferred that 32 percent of child-related ineligible EITC claimants in 1988 were responding to increases in the EITC (this figure includes all forms of noncompliance, including fraud) (Liebman, 1995a, pp. 26–27).

In another study, Liebman (1995b) matched 1990 tax returns with March 1991 CPS data to investigate the number and characteristics of EITC claimants who, based on the CPS data, did not have a qualifying child for EITC purposes in the household. His estimates from various subsamples indicated that 10 to 20 percent of taxpayers who claimed the EITC in 1990 did not have a qualifying child for EITC purposes. These findings should be interpreted with caution, however, because CPS data provide information about children in the household at a point in time and may not reflect the composition of the household during the previous tax year.

Hill, Hotz, Mullin, and Scholz (1997), described in the earlier section on participation, compared reports of income and family size across different data sets. Household income reported to tax authorities was quite consistent with income reported by employers to the state unemployment insurance system. Income reported by AFDC households to AFDC authorities, on the other hand, was underreported to a considerable degree: 36 to 69 percent of sample households with positive earnings in the state's unemployment insurance system in a given year underreported earnings to transfer program authorities (p. 32). The range reflects estimates in 1993 and 1994 as well as differences among one-and two-parent AFDC households, and among longer-term aid recipients and more recent entrants to AFDC. To gauge the degree to which reports of household size to different administrative authorities vary, the study compared the number of children in AFDC assistance units with number of dependents claimed on tax returns and find that these reports agreed for 57 to 80 percent of sample households (p. 28).

Hill, Hotz, Mullin, and Scholz also attempted to estimate the degree to which the AFDC households in their sample claimed the EITC but appeared ineligible for the credit. They found that 10 to 57 percent of the sample households were in this category, with an intermediate estimate around 25 percent (the range arises from using various eligibility definitions based on income source and number of children in the household; the intermediate estimate is drawn from one of these eligibility definitions, and is not necessarily a mid-point estimate). These estimates likely reflect biases and should be interpreted with caution, however, due to lack of coverage in the data on certain income sources and on presence of children during months a household does not receive AFDC.

Some Methodological Points. These studies can provide only rough estimates of the degree and causes of misreporting and fraudulent practices associated with inappropriate EITC claims, because researchers outside government cannot scrutinize returns or obtain access to confidential data that the IRS uses to identify ineligible claims or fraudulent behaviors. These researchers face a further challenge in gaining access to relevant data because a TCMP study has not been conducted since 1988, due to lack of Congressional funding. Important contributions of researchers are likely to involve identifying patterns or characteristics of ineligible claimants and estimating the degree to which noncompliance is associated with unintentional or intentional misreporting.

While concerns continue about misreports of income to maximize EITC benefits, the issue of greatest importance involves reporting of family responsibilities. Household membership of low-income households and caregiving responsibilities are difficult for tax authorities to ascertain. It is not at all clear, however, that providing income support through the tax system is necessarily prone to high levels of noncompliant behavior. About 95 percent of EITC claimants file a tax return for reasons other than claiming the credit (for example, they are required to file due to a tax liability, or they file to obtain a refund of overwithheld taxes) (Scholz, 1997, p. 6). Separating the causes and consequences of tax reporting behaviors motivated by noncompliance in response to EITC incentives and not to incentives in other parts of the tax code remains a difficult task.

Conclusion

As EITC benefits expand, workers face increasing incentives to change their labor market behaviors, by entering the labor market or adjusting their hours of work, to maximize benefits that the credit provides. At the same time, however, incentives increase for fraudulent behaviors that inappropriately take advantage of EITC benefits. Attempts to assess the credit's participation rate, labor market effects, and compliance must grapple with the difficult task of sorting out actual changes in behavior from changes in reporting these behaviors.

Costs associated with EITC noncompliance must be weighed along with other effects of the credit. In addition to estimating EITC participation and labor market effects, recent studies have examined other aspects of the credit including its impact on economic risk (Bird, 1996) and its impact on disposable money income and welfare (Browning, 1995). Furthermore, evaluating the appropriateness of the EITC for providing support to low-income households requires comparing various aspects of the credit with those of other mechanisms designed to assist low-income households. A recent study by Burkhauser, Couch, and Glenn (1996) makes such an attempt and examines the usefulness of the EITC in achieving policy goals traditionally attributed to the minimum wage.

The administrative and policy issues described in this paper, and the attempts that have been made to address these issues, suggest a future evaluation agenda that includes the following tasks: assessing various implementation aspects, including participation rates and administrative costs, that affect the efficiency with which the credit meets its stated goal of providing support to low-income households; obtaining timely, accurate estimates of the credit's labor market effects; identifying the degree to which taxpayer reporting behavior responds to EITC incentives as opposed to other incentives in the tax system; and measuring the scope and sources of EITC noncompliance and the characteristics associated with noncompliance.

Recent studies utilize linked administrative data to estimate the participation rate of the credit among low-income households, and to estimate the extent of possible noncompliant reporting to tax and transfer authorities. Future efforts likely will take advantage of increased efforts to link administrative and survey data, and may be able to identify further the effects of the credit on subpopulations of interest, such as low-income households on welfare. Use of instrumental variables, as in one recent study (Eissa and Hoynes, 1997), may produce more accurate estimates of the credit's labor market effects. Furthermore, the accessibility of adequate longitudinal data will encourage use of models such as the difference-in-differences approach that exploit expansions of the EITC and the increasing divergence of credit amounts for families with one child relative to families with two or more children. These strategies not only are particularly well suited for examining the fundamental administrative and policy issues of the EITC, but also provide models for examining other tax and transfer issues.

References

Bird, E. J. "Repairing the Safety Net: Is the EITC the Right Patch?" *Journal of Policy Analysis and Management,* 1996, *15* (1), 1–31.

Blank, R., and Ruggles, P. "When Do Women Use Aid to Families with Dependent Children and Food Stamps? The Dynamics of Eligibility Versus Participation," *Journal of Human Resources,* 1996, *31* (1), 57–89.

Browning, E. "Effects of the Earned Income Tax Credit on Income and Welfare." *National Tax Journal,* 1995, *48* (1), 23–43.

Burkhauser, R. V., Couch, K. A., and Glenn, A. J. "Public Policies for the Working Poor: The Earned Income Tax Credit Versus Minimum Wage Legislation." In S. W. Polachek (ed.), *Research in Labor Economics,* No. 15. Greenwich, Conn.: JAI Press, 1996.

Committee on Ways and Means, U.S. House of Representatives. *Green Book: Background Material and Data on Programs within the Jurisdiction of the Committee on Ways and Means.* Washington, D.C.: Government Printing Office, 1996.

Dickert, S., Houser, S., and Scholz, J. K. "The Earned Income Tax Credit and Transfer Programs: A Study of Labor Market and Program Participation." In J. Poterba (ed.), *Tax Policy and the Economy.* Cambridge, Mass.: MIT Press, 1995.

Eissa, N., and Hoynes, H. "The Earned Income Tax Credit and Labor Supply: Married Couples." Paper presented at the Joint Center for Poverty Research Workshop, Northwestern University, May 8, 1997.

Eissa, N., and Liebman, J. B. "Labor Supply Response to the Earned Income Tax Credit." *Quarterly Journal of Economics,* 1996, *111* (2), 605–637.

Hill, C. J., Hotz, V. J., Mullin, C. H., and Scholz, J. K. "EITC Eligibility, Participation and Compliance Rates for AFDC Households: Evidence from the California Caseload." Draft report prepared for the California Department of Social Services, May 1997.

Hoffman, S. D., and Seidman, L. S. "The Earned Income Tax Credit: Antipoverty Effectiveness and Labor Market Effects." Kalamazoo, Mich.: W. E. Upjohn Institute for Employment Research, 1990.

Liebman, J. B. *Noncompliance and the Earned Income Tax Credit: Taxpayer Error or Taxpayer Fraud?* Harvard University, Dec. 1995(a) (mimeo).

Liebman, J. B. *Who Are the Ineligible EITC Recipients?* Harvard University, Oct. 1995(b) (mimeo).

Meyer, B. D. "Natural and Quasi-Experiments in Economics," *Journal of Business and Economic Statistics,* 1995, *13* (2), 151–161.

Scholz, J. K. "The Earned Income Tax Credit: Participation, Compliance, and Antipoverty Effectiveness." *National Tax Journal,* 1994, *47* (1), 63–87.

Scholz, J. K., Deputy Assistant Secretary for Tax Analysis, U.S. Department of the Treasury. Testimony before the U.S. House of Representatives Committee on Ways and Means, May 8, 1997.

U.S. General Accounting Office. "Advance Payment Option is Not Widely Known or Understood by the Public." Washington, D.C., Feb. 1992. (GAO/GGD-92–26)

U.S. General Accounting Office. "Earned Income Tax Credit: Design and Administration Could Be Improved." Washington, D.C., Sept. 1993. (GAO/GGD-93–145)

U.S. Internal Revenue Service. *Study of EITC Filers for Tax Year 1994.* Apr. 1997.

CAROLYN J. HILL *is a Ph.D. student at Irving B. Harris Graduate School of Public Policy Studies, University of Chicago.*

V. JOSEPH HOTZ *is professor of economics and policy studies at University of California at Los Angeles.*

JOHN KARL SCHOLZ *is deputy assistant secretary, Tax Analysis, U.S. Department of the Treasury.*

Central issues in evaluating the Low-Income Housing Tax Credit are cost-effectiveness as the program stands; whether it adds to the supply of affordable housing; whether development costs of tax credit projects are reasonable relative to private, unsubsidized housing development; whether alternative means of achieving the objectives would be more efficient or be better targeted to lower-income households; and the feasibility of replacing the program with a directly budgeted subsidy. Methodological requirements for the evaluation include developing clear relationships among government costs, transaction costs, investor returns, and net equity provided to a project.

Evaluating the Low-Income Housing Tax Credit

James E. Wallace

What Is the Low-Income Housing Tax Credit?

The Low-Income Housing Tax Credit has become the primary vehicle for production of affordable rental housing in the United States. As an indication of the need for increasing the supply of affordable, physically adequate housing, consider the 8 million unsubsidized, extremely low-income renter households (less than 30 percent of area median income) in the United States. Although in 1993 3.6 million of these households lived in structurally adequate housing, they paid half or more of their incomes in rent. Most directly relevant to the housing supply question, another 818,000 lived in structurally inadequate units (Joint Center for Housing Studies, 1996, p. 22, based on the 1993 American Housing Survey). Incremental additions to the affordable housing stock through the public housing program have essentially ceased. Although block grant programs provide some direct support for the production of affordable housing, the only remaining federal program of any scale is the Low-Income Housing Tax Credit. It is particularly important, therefore, to assess the extent to which this program is making efficient use of the federal funds that are implicitly devoted to it through the tax code.

History. Section 42 of the Internal Revenue Code in the Tax Reform Act of 1986 created the Low-Income Housing Tax Credit (LIHTC). The original statute provided for a trial period, with a "sunset" in 1989 that was extended several times before being allowed to expire in 1992. Then, as part of the Revenue Reconciliation Act of 1993, the LIHTC was made a permanent part of the Internal Revenue Code. The LIHTC provides ten years of federal income tax credits to rental property owners who pledge to maintain at least a defined fraction of units at a restricted rent for lower income households for a period of time. It thus serves as a device to capture equity capital for affordable housing projects. Investors make up-front payments in order to claim the stream of tax credits, which are a direct reduction in the investors' federal income tax liability. Annual allocations of tax credits for potential projects are administered by housing agencies of states and territories (and by city agencies in New York and Chicago).

Mechanics. At this point a brief summary of mechanics of the LIHTC may assist the reader. The sequence is essentially the following:

Step 1. The IRS apportions annual credit available to state allocation agencies at $1.25 per capita.

Step 2. Developers apply for an allocation of tax credits based on a proposed project.

Step 3. Allocations are awarded competitively against agency priorities and scoring systems. In the Revenue Reconciliation Act of 1989, Congress required that the state allocating agencies give highest priority to projects "with the highest percentage of the housing credit dollars [used] for project costs other than the cost of intermediaries" and that they grant "no more than the amount of credit required to make the project feasible."

Step 4. Developers raise equity funds by marketing the tax credit benefits to investors, usually through a syndicator who collects a syndication fee, and seek conventional or concessionary financing (loans and grants) for the remaining costs of the project.

Step 5. Projects placed in service are awarded the credits appropriate to the type of project and the number of tax credit–eligible households to be served.

Step 6. Projects remaining in compliance generate tax benefits (annual credits against federal income tax liability for ten years) as the investors' return on equity.

Eligible Projects. Qualifying projects must serve households with income below the median for that area, although, technically, not every unit has to be occupied by a low-income family. To qualify a project, the developer must choose between a "set-aside" of at least 20 percent of the units for households with incomes at or below 50 percent of area median income, or at least 40 percent of units for households with incomes at or below 60 percent of area median income. Rents in qualifying units cannot exceed 30 percent of the elected income level (50 percent or 60 percent of area median income). In practice, most projects are set up so that 90 percent or more of the units are targeted to households within 60 percent of area median income.

Project investors receive the annual tax credit only if occupancy by households within the qualified income is maintained over a compliance period, which is a minimum of 15 years with a possible extension to 30 years.

If an owner fails to keep these terms, including providing the restricted rents for the reserved number of units set aside for low-income households, the tax credits are reduced accordingly. Further, if a project fails to continue to rent the agreed number of units to households under the income limit for the compliance period, the Internal Revenue Service can recapture from the owner a pro-rata portion of the credits already taken. This provides a powerful incentive for the owner to continue providing housing to households in the target income category for the full compliance period.

Compliance. Responsibility for compliance with the rules of the Low-Income Housing Tax Credit lies with the Internal Revenue Service, with the allocating agencies, and with the owner-investors. (See U.S. General Accounting Office, 1997, for a review of the Low-Income Housing Tax Credit.) In addition, projects with financing or assistance provided through HUD must satisfy a "subsidy layering review" as a requirement of the HUD Reform Act of 1989 (see Warren, Gorham, & Lamont, 1994).

The Internal Revenue Service is responsible for overseeing compliance, to ensure that the states and taxpayers use no more tax credits than authorized. The IRS requires annual reports from the states on their total tax credit allocations to proposed projects and their awards to individual projects when these projects are placed in service. Project owners must certify annually that the project has complied with the low-income set-aside requirements continuously over the period.

Allocating agencies have an obligation to ensure that no more credits are allocated than allowable and that the claims for credits are legitimate. The Internal Revenue Code requires that allocation agencies not award amounts in excess of the amounts necessary for financial feasibility and viability of the project. Allocation agencies are to consider sources and uses of funds and to evaluate (1) the reasonableness of development costs, (2) net income to be generated by the project and the debt service that could be supported with that net income, and (3) investment yield likely to be obtained when the tax credits are converted into equity investment (U.S. General Accounting Office, 1997, p. 73).

Developers are subject to competitive pressures in the proposal stage to satisfy agency priorities. In the operating phase of a project placed in service, the operators of the project are subject to an implicit pressure to keep the property in compliance so that the investors are not faced with a recapture of part of the tax credit benefits. This means ensuring that the income levels of the tenants and the rents charged meet the requirements agreed to and that the physical condition of the property is maintained.

Amount of the Annual Tax Credit. The annual amount of tax credit is a percentage of the "qualified basis," essentially all project development costs. The percentage is set nominally at either 9 percent or 4 percent, so as to yield a present value cost to the federal government of the ten-year stream of tax benefits of no more than, respectively: (1) 70 percent of the qualified basis for new construction or substantial rehabilitation, or (2) 30 percent of the qualified basis of acquisition costs of buildings that are substantially rehabilitated or are financed with federally subsidized loans, including tax-exempt bonds and the Section 515 Rural Rental Housing program. The U.S. Treasury periodically sets the percentages used to compute the annual tax credit amount that yield the 70 percent present value and the 30 percent value, depending on the yields of Treasury notes. Recent percentages for the annual amount of tax credit were 8.65 and 3.71 percent (Warren, Gorham, & Lamont, 1997b, p. 813).

As part of the Omnibus Reconciliation Act of 1989, Congress added provisions designed to increase LIHTC production in hard-to-serve areas by permitting projects in certain areas (metropolitan areas and non-metropolitan counties where construction, land, and utility costs are high relative to incomes or census tracts where at least 50 percent of the households have incomes less than 60 percent of the area median gross income) to claim a higher eligible basis (130 percent of the ordinary basis) for purposes of calculating the amount of the credit that can be provided. (See "Designation of Qualified Census Tracts and Difficult Development Areas: Notice," 1993.)

Impact on the Federal Budget. The 1986 legislation established an annual ceiling of $1.25 times the U.S. population for new credits to be allocated. This means that about $300 million in first-year credit authority can be allocated each year for new projects. Each year of allocation of $300 million to new projects in first-year credits implies that the potential total exposure to tax credits over the ten-year credit claim period is $3 billion. Also, if $300 million in first-year credits were awarded each year, by the end of ten years of uninterrupted availability of the tax credit, the annual amount of tax credits would accumulate to a steady state of $3 billion and remain at that level as projects reaching their tenth year of service would be succeeded by new projects. Actual numbers can be smaller if some of the available credits are not allocated or are allocated to potential projects that never are placed in service. The totals could also be larger if the population increased or if the $1.25 per capita rate were raised. Changing the annual ceiling on new credits or indexing it in some way would require further legislation. Also, tax credit projects financed with tax-exempt bonds are not limited by the tax credit cap, even though tax-exempt bonds have their own separate statutory cap.

The number of actual credits taken (tax liabilities offset) in a given year is thus a function of the cumulative number of projects actually placed in service and operating within their ten-year credit period. For the period 1997–2001 the Joint Committee on Taxation of the U.S. Congress estimated that the federal government would "spend" $17.9 billion on the Low-Income Housing Tax Credit. This estimated tax expenditure includes $2.8 billion for 1997 ($1.0 billion for corporations, $1.8 billion for individuals), rising to $4.5 billion in 2001 ($1.6 billion for corporations, $2.9 billion for individuals) (Warren, Gorham, & Lamont, 1997a, p. 562).

This may be an overestimate of actual tax credit expenditures, judging from the results of recent work by the U.S. General Accounting Office (1997) and a HUD contractor (Abt Associates Inc., 1996). According to the U.S. General Accounting Office, while annual per capita allocations total about $315 million each year, its data on projects actually placed in service indicate annual total tax credits in the range of $158 million in 1992 to $229 million in 1994. This would indicate ten-year total commitments of $1.58 billion for projects placed in service in 1992 and $2.29 billion for projects placed in service in 1994. The U.S. General Accounting Office requested an IRS study of the relationship between credits allocated in 1992 and credits awarded to projects placed in service. According to the results reported in the U.S. General Accounting Office study, $322 million in annual tax credits was allocated to projects in 1992; by 1994 only $161 million in credits, or about half of the amounts allocated, had actually been awarded to projects placed in service from the 1992 allocation cohort (p. 67). Some additional projects with 1992 allocations may have been placed in service later than 1994 and some allocations may have been returned and re-allocated to projects later placed in service.

Drawing on surveys from the National Council of State Housing Agencies, the Abt Associates Inc. study (1996) for HUD indicates an average of $255 million allocated each year to new projects during the period 1987–92, for an average of 86,580 low-income units each year, but the average number of units actually placed in service during the same period was 52,438, or about 60 percent of the amounts allocated. The data collected directly in the Abt study indicate an average of 59,253 units placed in service over the years 1993 and 1994.

These results taken together suggest a loss somewhere of perhaps 30 percent of the tax credits initially allocated. Quite possibly the necessary layers of concessionary financing simply do not materialize as projected at the application stage. Added to other normal challenges and delays in housing development, many planned projects simply may not happen. This suggests that, under closer monitoring of project proposals, more projects allocated tax credits could be completed and placed in service within the tax credit cap.

Results to Date. Precise figures on production of LIHTC units are not available, although estimates can be assembled from three sources already mentioned—results of a survey of members conducted by the National Council of State Housing Agencies (1995), a study conducted for HUD by Abt Associates Inc. (1996), and the review of the tax credit program conducted by the U.S. General Accounting Office (1997). A total number of LIHTC units placed in service since program inception through 1996 can be estimated as nearly six hundred thousand units, as follows:

1987–1992: 314,625 units (National Council of State Housing Agencies, 1995)
1993:   59,825 units (Abt Associates Inc., 1996, p. 3 – 2)
1994:   58,681 units (Abt Associates Inc., 1996, p. 3 – 2)
1995–96:   120,000 units at 60,000 units a year (author's estimate)
Total through 1996: 553,131 units

The cumulative number of tax credit units is thus rivaling the cumulative numbers of units produced under the HUD subsidized interest rate programs

(Section 236 and Section 221(d)(3) Below Market Interest Rate) of the 1960s and 1970s that produced 794,000 units, or the project-based Section 8 New Construction and Substantial Rehabilitation rental assistance program of the 1970s and 1980s that produced 362,000 units, or the Section 515 interest-subsidized rural rental housing program that produced 450,000 units by 1993. Virtually all Section 515 projects developed since 1987 use the tax credit, too (production figures tabulated in Wallace, 1995, p. 790).

What Are the Central Issues in Evaluating the Low-Income Housing Tax Credit?

The criteria for evaluating the Low-Income Housing Tax Credit include the following:

- Is the tax system the most *cost-effective* means to address the objectives of the tax credit?
- Does the housing produced under the tax credit program constitute a net addition to the *housing supply?*
- Are tax credit projects built for *development costs* as low as costs of projects built under market forces, rather than administrative controls?
- Are the objectives of the tax credit program good policy or are there more efficient *alternative means* of providing affordable housing better directed to those most in need?
- If the Low-Income Housing Tax Credit were *replaced with a direct funding mechanism,* how would efficiencies and administrative costs be affected?
- How politically feasible would such an approach be?

  Cost-Effectiveness of the Tax Credit Mechanism Itself. Suppose that the public policy objective is to produce exactly what the tax credit program is producing and to provide housing affordable to households under 60 percent of median income. Further suppose that the explicit development costs of producing this housing are what would be required no matter how financed. A fundamental evaluation measure would be the relationship between funds raised for actual development and the government costs of the tax credit. Because of the structure and complexity of the tax credit incentive, only a fraction of the present value to the government of the costs of the tax credit is delivered to the project for actual costs of development. This section provides a simplified overview of the structure of tax credit investments, how large they are, and how they relate to the amounts of tax credit provided.

  Typically, investors provide up-front payments representing the present value to these investors of the ten-year stream of tax credits discounted at the market rate of return. Tax credit investors typically do not purchase the credits for their full ten-year amount, because the tax credits are future returns and because actually realizing these tax credits is not certain. In practice, the investors' payments, termed *equity payments,* are phased over a period of several years in order to increase the total amount of equity paid. A delay in making outlays is worth something to investors. However, the usual rule of thumb for tax credit pricing simply uses the total equity payment, regardless of timing, in computing the equity investment.

This chapter uses the term *relative investment* to refer to the total investment (before subtracting out syndication and transaction costs) relative to total tax credits, that is (gross equity)/(total tax credits), where total tax credits means the simple arithmetic sum of ten years of annual tax credits. The general measure used to quantify yield is the *tax credit price,* defined as the ratio of the total amount of equity investment made in a project, net of syndication and transaction costs, or net equity to the total tax credits.

In its recent review of the tax credit the U.S. General Accounting Office (1997) obtained information on the price of tax credits. The study showed for a sample of properties placed in service from 1992 through 1994 that the tax credit equity price was less than 40 cents per dollar of total tax credit amount for 9 percent of projects, between $0.40 and $0.50 for 39 percent, between $0.50 and $0.60 for 32 percent, between $0.60 and $0.70 for 10 percent, and more than $0.70 for 8 percent of projects (p. 90). According to the U.S. General Accounting Office's sources, the average price increased from around $0.45 in 1987 to over $0.60 in 1996, owing partly to market competition and partly to a shift to corporate investors not subject to the limitations placed on individual investors (pp. 90, 91).

Table 3.1 provides a summary of the range of relationships between the tax credit amounts, the amounts actually available for development, and the effective government cost of the tax credits. Table 3.1 illustrates a range in equity investment returns from 7.5 percent to 20 percent, and shows that the relative investment (gross equity/total tax credits) would vary from $0.68 per dollar of ten years' worth of tax credits at a 7.5 percent return to $0.42 per dollar at a 20 percent return.

Because of the legal and accounting services that must be used to "syndicate" the tax credit investment to interested buyers (market them to and administer them for individual and corporate limited partners) and the costs involved in monitoring the project for the investors as well as funding reserves to assure project viability, the actual amount delivered to a project for its development costs is reduced. Phased payments of the equity investment can maximize the total equity investment and contribute to the eligible basis, but may require bridge financing to provide the capital to the project when it is needed. The expense of the bridge financing is another cost to be deducted from the total equity investment, although the conventional terminology for price does not subtract these bridge financing costs from the gross equity in arriving at net equity. Syndication costs can range from about 10 percent to about 25 percent of the amount invested.

Table 3.1 illustrates the effects of this range. If syndication costs are as little as 10 percent of the invested amounts (gross equity), then the net equity delivered to the project is on the order of 55 percent of the ten-year credit total at an investor's rate of return of 10 percent. However, at syndication costs of 25 percent of the gross equity, the net equity drops to only 46 percent of the

Table 3.1. Tax Credit Relationships

Rate of Return	Relative Investment (Gross Equity/ Total Credit)	"Price" (Net Equity/ Total Credit)	Net Equity/ (Government PV Credit)
Where Syndication Costs/Gross Equity = 10%			
20.0%	41.9%	37.7%	48.5%
15.0	50.2	45.2	58.1
12.5	55.4	49.8	64.1
10.0	61.4	55.3	71.1
7.5	68.6	61.8	79.4
Where Syndication Costs/Gross Equity = 15%			
20.0%	41.9%	35.6%	45.8%
15.0	50.2	42.7	54.8
12.5	55.4	47.1	60.5
10.0	61.4	52.2	67.2
7.5	68.6	58.3	75.0
Where Syndiation Costs/Gross Equity = 20%			
20.0%	41.9%	33.5%	43.1%
15.0	50.2	40.2	51.6
12.5	55.4	44.3	56.9
10.0	61.4	49.2	63.2
7.5	68.6	54.9	70.6
Where Syndicaton Costs/Gross Equity = 25%			
20.0%	41.9%	31.4%	40.4%
15.0	50.2	37.6	48.4
12.5	55.4	41.5	53.4
10.0	61.4	46.1	59.3
7.5	68.6	51.5	66.2

Definitions:

B = basis (roughly the development of cost)

AC = annual credit

= 0.09 basis (9% adjusted to yield GPV of 70% of basis)

TC = total credit = $10 \cdot AC$

S = syndication costs

R = investor rate of return

I = investment (total of investor payments, up-front), or gross equity

= $PV(AC, R, 10)$

GPV = government present value of ten-year tax credit

= $PV(AC, \text{government rate}, 10)$

= $0.7 \cdot \text{basis}$ (by legislation)

Then relative invesment = gross equity/total credit

= $PV(AC, R, 10)/(10 \cdot AC)$

Net equity/total credit = "Price"

= $(1 - S/I) \cdot PV(AC, R, 10)/(10 \cdot AC)$

Net equity/ (government present value of ten-year tax credit) = $(1 - S/I) \cdot AC \cdot PV(1, R, 10)/GPV$

= $(1 - S/I) \cdot 0.09B \cdot PV(1, R, 10)/0.7B$

= $(0.09/0.7) \cdot (1 - S/I) \cdot PV(1, R, 10)$

ten-year credit amount even for an investor willing to settle for a 10 percent return. An investment firm handling tax credit investments indicated in 1996 that after-tax returns on Low-Income Housing Tax Credit projects had dropped from the range of 14 to 15 percent in the early 1990s to current levels of around 10 to 11 percent (Warren, Gorham, & Lamont, 1996). By asking firms involved in the syndication process, the U.S. General Accounting Office study (1997, p. 82) found that the range of syndication fees is from 10 to 27 percent of the equity raised.

A number of nonprofit tax credit equity funds have been created to reduce to a minimum the transaction costs involved in assembling tax credit investments. These include the National Equity Fund of the Local Initiatives Support Corporation (LISC) and the Enterprise Social Investment Corporation of the Enterprise Foundation. States and municipalities also have set up equity funds, including the Massachusetts Housing Investment Corporation and the Chicago Equity Fund. The price of the tax credit investment is a function of the investor's after-tax rate of return (essentially the return required in the market by the marginal buyer of a syndication offering) and the relative cost of syndication and transaction costs. The finding by the U.S. General Accounting Office (1997, p. 90) that average prices have increased to over $0.60 per ten years' worth of tax credits implies a rate of return on the tax credit investment of just under 10 percent combined with syndication costs of just under 10 percent of gross equity.

Effective rates of return can be higher than those shown in Table 3.1 for investors able to use the property depreciation to shelter other income from tax and for those making phased payments. The Equity Program of the Massachusetts Housing Investment Corporation (1996, p. 11) recently reported that it is able to deliver 69 cents of equity funds as net proceeds, net of syndication and transaction costs, for every dollar of total, ten-year tax credit amount. Cummings and DiPasquale (1998) recently completed a study of over 2,500 LIHTC developments built between 1987 and 1996 and provide a detailed investigation of trends in gross equity, net equity, and internal rates of return on LIHTC projects.

Government costs of tax credits are assessed in present-value terms as well as in the undiscounted ten-year sum. When the legislation was adopted, the 9 percent credit available for new construction was intended to produce a present value of tax credit costs to the federal government of 70 percent of the eligible basis of a project, computed at a discount rate equal to an average rate of return on Treasury securities. In the 1992–94 period the average government discount rate was 6.7 percent. A ten-year stream of tax credits computed as 9 percent of eligible basis would discount to 70 percent of basis at 6.71 percent. Government costs for a "9 percent" project are thus not viewed as the simple, arithmetic sum of the ten-year credit but as the smaller, present value amount.

The present value cost-to-government of tax credits is not delivered as net equity to the project, however. The last column in Table 3.1 illustrates the percentage of government present value of credit costs that are delivered as net equity (investment total based on market return for investors, less syndication costs) to the project. For example, for a tax credit project marketed to investors willing to accept a 10 percent return, the percentage of government present value delivered as net equity is about 71 percent at syndication costs of 10 percent but drops to 59 percent for syndication costs of 25 percent (of the ten-year tax credit total). While the investment market sets the investors' rate of return as a function of the tax rate structure and the perceived riskiness of the investment, the allocation agencies are left to administrative procedures to try to maximize the amount of investment actually delivered to the project.

It is clear from this discussion that the net proceeds of tax credit investment (net equity) actually delivered for project costs are likely to be in the range of 60 to 70 percent of the present value of the credits to the government. The implication is that less is available to finance the project than the effective cost to government to provide the subsidy. The two major sources of loss are that the investors discount the credits at a higher rate than the government, and that raising capital in this way incurs the costs of syndication to provide the legal, accounting, and investment management services to market the credits to the investment community and manage the administration of the tax credits. This inherent inefficiency has been recognized since nearly the beginning of the program. Early U.S. General Accounting Office testimony (1989, 1990) outlined the losses in the form of the "risk premium" demanded by investors, relative to the government's present value cost of the credits, and the large fraction of the investment funds raised that are used for transaction costs.

Regarding syndication fees, the Internal Revenue Code requires agencies to consider the amount of funds to be generated by the tax credits and whether a project maximizes the portion that is used for project costs other than for intermediaries, essentially the syndicators who raise equity capital for housing projects. The U.S. General Accounting Office (1997, p. 82) found that syndication fees absorbed a range of 10 to 27 percent of the funds raised from investors, as mentioned above. This is the most directly identifiable cost arising purely from the use of the tax credit as the device to capture capital.

We will return later to the question of whether the tax credit could be replaced with a simpler, directly budgeted system with fewer losses but provide the same result that the current tax credit program is providing. However, measurement of the cost-effectiveness of the mechanism itself is relatively straightforward. The conclusion is that the tax credit is not a cost-effective delivery mechanism.

Adding to the Supply of Affordable Housing. Consider the objective of the tax credit program in adding to the long-term supply of affordable housing through new, or substantially rehabilitated, housing units at restricted rents. One question is whether the units produced through subsidy incentives are a net addition to the housing stock. This is an old question, never satisfactorily answered. An investigation in progress at the University of Wisconsin on the Low-Income Housing Tax Credit suggests that over the period 1987 through 1993 tax credit units were substituting one-for-one for production of unsubsidized multifamily construction, based on an econometric model of factors affecting housing supply at the state level (Malpezzi and Vandell, 1996).

Even if this were so, one could argue that a public policy objective is achieved in locating the projects where they are needed to provide affordable housing and in targeting these units to lower-income households than they otherwise would have been offered to. However, for tax credit projects in which existing property is acquired and rehabilitated, it is quite possible that this actually directly reduces the supply of housing affordable to the poor if the rents in the rehabilitated tax credit project are higher than the previous rents of the building acquired.

The tentative answer to the question posed about whether the LIHTC leads to a net addition to housing supply appears to be that it may not. More complete research needs to be done on this issue, and we will still be faced with the question of whether an unfettered market allocation of multifamily housing units, perhaps combined with tenant-based assistance, could accomplish the same public policy objectives at less cost.

Development Costs. Information on sources and uses of funds in tax credit projects is available from three national studies: a study for HUD by ICF on projects placed in service between 1987 and 1989 (ICF Inc., 1991); a study for HUD by Abt Associates on costs and sources of funds for nonprofit-sponsored housing development, of which twelve of fifteen were tax credit projects (Hebert and others, 1993); and the study by the U.S. General Accounting Office on improving controls over tax credits (1997).

The ICF study presents results from its developer survey in terms of costs per unit, includes syndication costs as a project development cost, and does not identify concessionary financing. Average gross equity ($12,722) represents 29 percent of total costs. If syndication costs are removed from both sources and costs, net equity ($12,722 − $1,605) represents 26 percent of costs ($44,412 − $1,605) (1991, p. 12).

The study of nonprofit development costs and funding conducted for HUD by Abt Associates compiled information on twelve tax credit projects and three non–tax credit projects in five metropolitan areas. An important contribution of the Abt study for evaluation purposes is the careful, full accounting for both sources and uses of development resources. Eleven of the fifteen projects studied had debt financing from a bank or private financial institution, eight received debt funding from a state housing finance agency, and fourteen got loans from the municipality (in most cases using Community Development Block Grant or HOME funds). Because filling the financing gap is a challenge for virtually every tax credit project, the number of financing sources becomes quite large, itself contributing to project costs in the form of multiple negotiations and closings. The number of financing sources required averaged 7.8 and ranged from 5 to 11.

Table 3.2 collapses financing sources for full development costs into syndication proceeds, first mortgage loan, other loans, grants, and non-cash resources. The overall average full development cost was $125,206 per unit,

Table 3.2. Estimates on Tax Credit Project Sources and Uses of Funds: Abt Study (Purposive Sample of Fifteen Properties Placed in Service 1990–1992; Twelve Were Tax Credit Projects)

Sources/Uses of Funds	Average Across All 12 Developments	Low End: Blue Hill Homes (Kansas City)	High End: Langham Court Cooperative (Boston)
I. Sources of funds (financing per unit)			
Syndication proceeds	$34,275	$15,436	$50,893
First mortgage loan	47,992	15,000	118,982
Other loans	12,917	15,212	0
Grants	8,425	6	34,994
Non-cash resources	21,598	2,029	59,795
TOTAL	125,206	47,682	264,664
II. Uses of funds (use per unit)			
Planning and design	$3,597	$886	$9,287
Acquisition	14,861	5,534	10,696
Finance/carrying charges	8,468	1,634	26,196
Relocation	609	0	0
Construction	70,521	32,063	137,443
Real estate taxes	541	71	773
Marketing	285	0	1,010
Reserves	3,435	322	3,899
Legal and organization (including development consultants)	2,145	1,273	6,878
Developer's overhead/staff	2,566	281	8,075
Developer's fee	12,542	706	49,847
Syndication costs	5,637	4,913	10,560
TOTAL	$125,206	47,682	264,664

Note: The average per-unit figures across the twelve tax credit projects in the Abt study were computed by summing costs across the projects and dividing by the total number of units in the projects. These are *not* population characteristics for tax credit projects completed during the period 1990 to 1992 but simple averages from a non-random sample.

Source: Hebert and others, 1993, Volume II, Case Studies.

although the range in costs was large across the twelve tax credit projects, from a high of $264,664 to a low of $47,682 per unit. Syndication costs were 16 percent of syndication proceeds overall; direct construction costs amounted to only 56 percent of full development costs; non-cash resources covered 17 percent of full development costs (percentages not shown in the table).

The 1997 U.S. General Accounting Office study provided data from a national probability sample of 423 tax credit developments, from which owner responses were received on 380 projects on the costs of tax credit projects and the role of tax credits in financing these low-income housing developments. On the basis of the sample, the U.S. General Accounting Office (p. 75) estimated that tax credit projects placed in service in the period 1992 through 1994 cost a total of about $10.7 billion to develop: about $5.8 billion in construction expenses; about $2.7 billion in construction-related fees, such as those paid to developers and builders; and about $2.2 billion in other costs, including the costs of acquiring the property. The equity investment raised through the award of tax credits ($3.1 billion) amounts to about one-third of the total development costs of the projects sampled, commercial mortgage loans about one-third, and concessionary financing in some form about another third (p. 76).

Concessionary financing is necessary because, in a typical project, the restricted rents generate only enough revenue over and above operating expenses to pay for the debt service on about one-third of the costs of the project. It helps that the tax credit equity covers another third of project costs, but that still leaves a large gap. The upshot is that developers must seek grants, donated land or services, or loans at concessionary terms (low interest rates or deferred repayment) in order to complete the financing of the project. The U.S. General Accounting Office estimated that 69 percent of the tax credit projects placed in service between 1992 and 1994 required subsidies in addition to tax credits, amounting to about $3 billion in concessionary loans or grants. Among these projects concessionary loans or grants provided 37 percent of the financing for these projects (p. 87).

Much of the concessionary financing (loans or grants) noted in the U.S. General Accounting Office study comes from locally administered federal block grant programs (Community Development Block Grant or the HOME Investment Partnership Program) or from the interest-subsidized financing of the Section 515 program administered by the Rural Housing Service. Besides concessionary loans and grants, tax credit projects may receive rental subsidies for the operating side that effectively lower the capital financing required for the projects to meet the rental restrictions for low-income tenants. The U.S. General Accounting Office estimated from its sample that tax projects placed in service between 1992 and 1994 received about $229 million a year in combined project-based and tenant-based rental assistance payments. With this type of assistance considered, the percentage of tax credit projects in the U.S. General Accounting Office study with assistance beyond tax credits increases to 86 percent (p. 87).

For the tax credit projects that have been produced, one evaluation question is whether the costs of the projects have been competitive with similar housing produced by normal market forces. Section 42 of the Internal Revenue Code requires the state allocating agencies to consider the "reasonableness" of project development costs when determining the amount of tax credits necessary for project feasibility, but does not provide criteria for determining reasonableness. One reason this flexibility was left to states was the awareness among members of Congress of the difficulty of establishing cost limits that would reflect the wide range of development conditions and housing needs that might be addressed with the tax credit program. The 1997 U.S. General Accounting Office report focuses primarily on the issue of how the allocating agencies have gone about reviewing cost elements and establishing controls over them.

In a June 1993 report and an October 1995 pamphlet on best practices, the National Council of State Housing Agencies (NCSHA) has tried to provide guidance to its members on cost controls and guidelines for tax credit projects. NCSHA suggested a baseline standard for costs using the limits of the HUD Section 221(d)(3) mortgage insurance program. The HUD program is designed to establish maximum per-unit cost limits equivalent to the costs of constructing nonluxury multifamily housing projects for different areas within each state. The limits were initially set by Congress in legislation and are adjusted annually by HUD to reflect changes in construction costs. The limits provide different maximums according to the mix of number of bedrooms and building type (elevator and non-elevator buildings).

According to the U.S. General Accounting Office report (1997, p. 78), forty-eight of the fifty-four allocating agencies surveyed reported that they have established guidelines for controlling overall construction costs, including twenty-two that said they employ the dollar-specific limits of the 221(d)(3) guidelines. Although no comparisons with these guidelines were made, the U.S. General Accounting Office, in its sample of projects placed in service between 1992 and 1994, found average development costs of $60,000 per unit ($68,000 for new construction and $48,000 for rehabilitation). Project development costs included land acquisition, building acquisition and/or construction costs, builders' overhead and profit, and financing costs. It is not clear from the U.S. General Accounting Office report whether developers' fees were included. About 10 percent of the units cost less than $20,000, two-thirds cost under $60,000, and about 10 percent cost more than $100,000 (pp. 49–50).

In the Abt study (1996) of nonprofit-sponsored tax credit projects for HUD, actual construction costs per square foot were compared with location-adjusted costs from R. S. Means (1991). Tax credit project construction costs were found to vary from 19 percent under R. S. Means costs to 20 percent above, with an average of 6.7 percent above, based on the six new construction tax credit projects examined in the study (Hebert and others, 1993, pp. 5–12). As noted in the study, a number of factors could contribute to differences other than inefficiencies or developer-inflated costs. These factors could include unit size (units may be larger or smaller than average with attendant differences from relatively fixed-cost items like bathroom and kitchen plumbing); subsurface conditions; variations in building code requirements; site and neighborhood conditions; and central city development conditions, such as cramped lot sizes and the need for round-the-clock security, that differ from metro-average conditions.

The 1997 U.S. General Accounting Office study also addressed other components of development cost, including developer fees, fees to builders and related parties, and syndication fees. Among the fifty-four agencies surveyed by the U.S. General Accounting Office, developer fee limits ranged from 10 to 23 percent, but on varying bases. The National Council of State Housing Agencies

(1993, p. 158) had recommended that developer fees be limited to 15 percent of total development costs, and that fees to builders not exceed 14 percent of construction costs. The U.S. General Accounting Office (1997) found that about half the agencies followed the NCSHA recommendation fairly closely and others introduced variations.

Unfortunately, the evaluation question posed, "Are tax credit projects built for development costs as low as costs of projects built under market forces, rather than administrative controls?" cannot be satisfactorily answered. More research is needed that deals with the development costs of the buildings produced under the tax credit, controlling for what is actually produced, where, and under what adverse development conditions. It might be possible to address this through econometric models, if large enough samples were available with adequate data. At least it would be instructive to see a careful and independent analysis of construction and development costs by conventional development standards, done at a "due diligence" level on a fairly large group of tax credit projects.

Alternative Means. Addressing the issue of alternatives to the Low-Income Housing Tax Credit, one needs to examine both the production issue and the question of who (particularly, at what income level) is served by the tax credit program. Nelson (1994) has argued that the effective subsidy provided by the tax credit does not reach the neediest households, which is a way of noting that the program, as it was designed, was not targeted to these households but requires additional subsidies to do so. The question arises whether these additional subsidies are best spent in tax credit projects or elsewhere.

Public housing is the primary federal program for constructing housing for low-income households provided at rents limited to a percentage of household income. (The Low-Income Housing Tax Credit program limits rents but does not limit the percentage of a particular household's income paid for rent.) As of 1985, about 80 percent of public housing households had incomes below 50 percent of their area's median income, based on unpublished Abt Associates Inc. data from their Public Housing Modernization Needs Study, conducted for HUD in 1985 (686 responses from a survey of 818 public housing agencies). As of 1996, the U.S. General Accounting Office estimated from its sample that about three-fourths of qualifying households in the tax credit properties had incomes at or below 50 percent of their area's median income (U.S. General Accounting Office, 1997, pp. 39–40). However, 71 percent of the qualifying households benefitted directly or indirectly from other types of housing assistance besides tax credits.

How would costs compare if tax credit projects were to serve the same income levels as public housing? U.S. General Accounting Office testimony in 1993 provided comparisons based on nine public housing agencies that had both developed regular public housing and sponsored development of tax credit projects. Their comparison found that: tax credit projects serve more elderly, but fewer large families; tax credit projects need operating subsidies to serve tenants as poor as public housing tenants; tax credit projects more often were located in low-income and minority areas (largely because, unlike the tax credit program, public housing agencies are prohibited from developing additional public housing in neighborhoods that already contain a high percentage of federally subsidized households or minority households); and tax credits are a more expensive way to serve households with similar incomes. A case study of a Maryland public housing agency compared the costs to the federal government of developing and operating the public housing and tax credit projects during their first fifteen years. Using a discounted present value analysis, the public housing costs were found to be $72,000 per unit and the tax credit project costs to serve the tenants with the same income levels as the public housing project $91,000 per unit (U.S. General Accounting Office, 1993, pp. 6–7).

A more radical approach is to compare the tax credit program with direct tenant assistance, like the federal Section 8 rental assistance program for existing housing, often termed "housing vouchers." A comparison with vouchers assumes that enough physically adequate housing within the rent limits of the assistance program is available within a reasonable search period—that is, that there is no housing supply issue—and dismisses the difficult-to-monetize possible community revitalization benefits of particular tax credit projects. The tax credit study performed for HUD by ICF computed the fifteen-year discounted stream of federal costs for tax credit projects and for housing vouchers providing the difference between 30 percent of the incomes of the tenants in the tax credit projects and the local Fair Market Rent established by HUD. Neither computation included administrative costs. The results indicate that projects depending on the credit only, with tenants at relatively higher income levels, have costs of 1.8 times the voucher costs. Tax credit projects using the Section 515 program had discounted costs 2.3 times the discounted voucher costs. Projects with various other federal, state, or local subsidies, such as CDBG grants or loans, served a relatively high income level, had high capital costs and operating subsidies, and yielded a ratio of 5.9 times the voucher costs (ICF Inc., 1991).

A 1992 staff memorandum of the Congressional Budget Office (CBO) developed a largely theoretical argument about the superiority of a housing voucher approach relative to the tax credit. More recently, in its 1997 report to Congress on revenue and spending options for reducing the deficit, the Congressional Budget Office found that housing assistance could be provided to the same number of people at lower cost if the assistance was provided in the form of an expanded housing voucher program. The CBO noted arguments by advocates that affordable housing meeting minimal standards is in short supply for low-income residents in some areas and that housing construction is needed as part of neighborhood revitalization in some areas. The CBO's counter is that the high overhead costs of the tax credit make some housing subsidized by the tax credit even more expensive to produce and rent than would otherwise be the case. The tax credit subsidizes only new and substantially rehabilitated housing, which is inherently more expensive than the existing housing meeting minimum standards of habitability subsidized by vouchers. Moreover, the CBO pointed out, the LIHTC is expensive because of the high rates of return required by private investors to compensate for the risks of such investments and the high administrative and marketing costs in organizing low-income housing syndicates, which average 20 percent in some cases.

In any attempt to switch to housing vouchers the federal resources now directed to the LIHTC, a fundamental limitation lies in the federal budget constraints on "discretionary" spending. "The discretionary spending limits of the Balanced Budget and Emergency Deficit Control Act of 1985 (as amended in 1990 and 1993) already impose severe constraints on funding for existing discretionary programs. Expanding the housing voucher program would subject those programs to even greater budgetary pressures" (Congressional Budget Office, 1997).

Replacement with a Direct Subsidy.   Could the equity capital raised by the tax credit be replaced with a direct capital grant? The idea of replacing tax subsidies with direct subsidies is not a new one. For example, the Congressional Budget Office in 1977 reviewed real estate tax shelters and considered direct subsidy alternatives. Stegman (1991) suggested that the tax credit could be replaced with a direct capital grant for affordable housing development at about half the cost. The primary appeal of replacing the tax credit with a direct grant would be the virtual elimination of the syndication costs. Further, the loss from investors requiring a higher return than government discount rates would be eliminated. A direct grant would provide one dollar instead of the 60 or 70 cents on the dollar of discounted federal costs now delivered. (See Table 3.1.) If the effective amount of federal expenditures were to remain the same as the tax expenditures under the current system, either more projects could be subsidized under current rules on incomes and rents or deeper subsidies could be tied to lower rent levels and reach further down in the income distribution.

A major question would remain regarding incentives to maintain the low-income character of the project over at least a fifteen-year period. At present, investors are subject to a recapture by the IRS of part of the tax benefits already taken, if, over the required period, the project fails to provide decent housing to households of the contracted income levels. This recapture penalty is a significant incentive to maintain compliance. In a direct capital grant system, it would theoretically be possible to construct a binding contractual requirement for compliance and money penalties for failure. What is less clear is whether these penalties would be as collectible from a limited partnership as the recapture of tax benefits that are now due the IRS for failure to comply under the current system.

As a general matter, substituting a direct up-front grant for the tax credit raises questions of administration and budget scrutiny. The fact that most tax-favored investments have required no direct administration has been used as an argument in their favor and as a criticism that the benefits are not necessarily well targeted. However, in the case of the Low-Income Housing Tax

Credit, a quite developed administrative apparatus already exists in the allocating agencies, and the same mechanism serves to target the benefits.

Administration of a direct grant could be accomplished by the same agencies now administering the allocation of tax credits through precisely the same mechanism of priorities and competition in applications to the tax credit allocation agencies and their monitoring of compliance. No additional administrative costs would be involved. These costs are now essentially capitalized into development costs and could be treated the same way under a direct capital grant. HUD might continue to monitor the subsidy layering issue, but the costs of IRS compliance monitoring would be eliminated.

Would a direct capital grant be more vulnerable to budget pressures and year-to-year appropriations than the tax credit? As an on-budget item, it would be subject to all the scrutiny and trading that goes on within the budget process, as alluded to in the 1997 CBO report to Congress. However, in some sense, the Congress has almost treated the tax credit as an on-budget item since its inception. It was enacted for a finite period, voted one-year extensions, allowed to lapse in 1992, reinstated then threatened with cancellation in the 1996 budget, only to be preserved as "permanent." In 1996 Congressman Bill Archer (R–Texas), chairman of the Ways and Means Committee, at first indicated that he wanted to see the program canceled in the wake of indications, later withdrawn, from the IRS that there was widespread fraud and abuse in the program. So it is not clear that the level and frequency of scrutiny of a direct capital grant program would be that different from the attention paid to the current tax credit.

Then there would be the political issue of admitting to providing development grants to for-profit entities. A large fraction of the tax credit projects now developed are sponsored by nonprofit organizations. Providing grants to nonprofits in lieu of tax credits would not be politically problematic. It would be quite parallel to the Section 202 senior/handicapped housing program, or the public housing development program, in which direct federal grants actually cover essentially all of the capital costs, not just a fraction. The outright for-profit entities now developing tax credit projects clearly receive federal benefits through the tax code, but it might be politically more difficult, though ultimately more cost-effective, to do this openly through direct appropriations of federal funds. Furthermore, many would argue that such a switch would not be seamless and would lead to another learning curve of several years before production levels of affordable housing were restored.

The answer to the evaluation question about alternative means is that tenant-based subsidies would be cheaper where alternative, physically adequate, affordable housing is available. The argument that production subsidies for affordable housing are justifiable based on positive neighborhood impacts still lacks clear measures and empirical data on potential positive neighborhood impacts of tax credit construction that might justify the costs of construction in particular situations. A direct-funding mechanism that addresses the major requirements of the tax credit program appears to be possible in principle. The political feasibility of the direct-funding approach appears to be beyond questions of evaluation.

References

Abt Associates Inc. *Development and Analysis of the National LIHTC Database, Final Report.* Cambridge, Mass.: Abt Associates Inc., 1996. (Prepared for U.S. Department of Housing and Urban Development.)

Congressional Budget Office. "The Cost-Effectiveness of the Low-Income Housing Tax Credit Compared with Housing Vouchers." CBO Staff Memorandum, April 1992.

Congressional Budget Office. "Rev-29, Chapter Six: Repeal the Low-Income Housing Tax Credit." *In Reducing the Deficit: Spending and Revenue Options.* Washington, D.C.: March 1997.

Congressional Budget Office. *Real Estate Tax Shelter Subsidies and Direct Subsidy Alternatives.* Washington, D.C.: May 1997.

Cummings, J,. and DiPasquale, D. *Building Affordable Rental Housing: An Analysis of the Low-Income Housing Tax Credit.* Boston, Massachusetts: City Research, 1998.

"Designation of Qualified Census Tracts and Difficult Development Areas: Notice." *Federal Register,* April 15, 1993, 58 (71), 19, 704–19, 765.

Hebert, S., and others. *Nonprofit Housing: Costs and Funding.* Vol. I: *Findings,* Vol. II: *Case Studies.* (HUD-1435-PDR (I) and (II), November 1993). Washington, D.C.: Department of Housing and Urban Development, 1993.

ICF Inc. *Evaluation of the Low-Income Housing Tax Credit.* Fairfax (now located in Vienna), Va.: ICF Inc., 1991.

Joint Center for Housing Studies. *The State of the Nation's Housing.* Cambridge, Mass.: Harvard University, The Joint Center for Housing Studies, 1996.

Malpezzi, S., and Vandell, K. *Evaluation of the Low Income Housing Tax Credit: Interim Report.* Unpublished paper, School of Business, University of Wisconsin, Madison, January 24, 1996 (Working Draft 95–15).

Massachusetts Housing Investment Corporation. *1996 Annual Report.* Boston: Massachusetts Housing Investment Corporation, 1996.

Means, R. S. *Means Square Foot Costs.* Kingston, Mass.: The R.S. Means Company, 1991.

National Council of State Housing Agencies. *State HFA Handbook: 1994 NCSHA Annual Survey Results.* Washington, D.C.: National Council of State Housing Agencies, 1995.

Nelson, K. P. "Whose Shortage of Affordable Housing?" *Housing Policy Debate,* 1994, 5 (4), 401–442.

Stegman, M. A. "The Excessive Cost of Creative Financing: Growing Inefficiencies in the Production of Low-Income Housing." *Housing Policy Debate,* 1991, 2 (2), 357–373.

U.S. General Accounting Office. *Costs Associated with Low-Income Housing Tax Credit Partnerships.* Fact sheet for the Chairman, Subcommittee on Ways and Means, House of Representatives. July 1989. (GAO/GGD-89–100FS)

U.S. General Accounting Office. "Low-Income Housing Tax Credit Utilization and Syndication." Statement before the Subcommittee on HUD/Moderate Rehabilitation Investigations Committee on Banking, Housing, and Urban Affairs, United States Senate. April 27, 1990. (GAO/T-RCED-90–73)

U.S. General Accounting Office. "Projects Developed with Low-Income Housing Tax Credit Differ from Traditional Public Housing Development Projects." Testimony before the Subcommittee on Housing and Community Development, Committee on Banking, Finance and Urban Affairs, House of Representatives. June 17, 1993. (GAO/T-RCED-93–54)

U.S. General Accounting Office. *Tax Credits: Opportunities to Improve Oversight of the Low-Income Housing Program.* March 1997. (GAO/GGD/RCED-97–55)

Wallace, J. E. "Financing Affordable Housing in the United States." *Housing Policy Debate,* 1995, 6 (4), 785–814.

Warren, Gorham, & Lamont. "Draft Subsidy Layering Guidelines Revise Calculations of Proceeds from Tax Credit Syndications." *Housing and Development Reporter,* 1994, 22, 386.

Warren, Gorham, & Lamont. "Resale Market for Tax Credits Going Strong, Syndicators Say." *Housing and Development Reporter,* 1996, 24, 170.

Warren, Gorham, & Lamont. "Tax Credit Program Cost Estimated at $17.9 Billion for Fiscal 1997–2001." *Housing and Development Reporter,* 1997, 24, 562.

Warren, Gorham, & Lamont. "Tax Credit Briefs." *Housing and Development Reporter,* 1997, 24, 813.

JAMES E. WALLACE *is a principal associate and vice president at Abt Associates Inc. in Cambridge, Massachusetts.*

A study of the impact of employee stock ownership plans on corporate performance illustrates the possibility of using tax data for a quasi-experimental design and some attendant evaluation issues.

Employee Stock Ownership Plans: Using Tax Data in a Quasi-Experimental Design

Terry J. Hanford

The history of employee stock ownership plans (ESOPs) is unusual. A grand theoretical vision does not find a home in federal tax law every day. Employee ownership in the form of ESOPs was largely inspired by the vision of San Francisco lawyer Louis Kelso. In *The Capitalist Manifesto* (1958), Kelso and his co-author, philosopher Mortimer Adler, blamed many economic ailments on the highly skewed distribution of stock ownership. According to Kelso and Adler, because most American workers did not own stock they constantly pressed for wage increases, which tended to be inflationary, and were unsympathetic toward profits, which were more beneficial to the economy's long-term health. They also believed the existing mechanisms for raising funds for business expansion tended to reinforce the concentration of ownership. As the title of their book implies, Kelso and Adler were concerned that unless workers could get a stake in the growth and success of the capitalist economy, they would be more susceptible to the lure of communism, which in the context of the 1950s was not a trivial consideration.

Kelso devised the ESOP as a way to make more workers stockholders and thereby imbue them with more sympathy toward the profit-making capitalist system. A major stumbling block was how to finance the purchase of stock by ordinary workers. Kelso's clever solution to this problem was to propose a

Although the evaluation described here was conducted by the U.S. General Accounting Office (GAO), the views and opinions expressed here are the author's and not the GAO's. Although the author had lead responsibility for the impact analysis, the project was a team effort.

"leveraging" arrangement in which a trust would obtain a bank loan to purchase newly issued shares in a firm on behalf of its employees. The loan would be paid off gradually with the income earned by the new capital this stock represented. In effect, Kelso had created a plan to give workers a share in new capital growth, and thus a stake in the capitalist system, without redistributing current capital ownership.

Kelso's ideas found little application until after he was introduced to Louisiana Senator Russell Long in 1973. At that time, the Senator was chairman of the Senate Committee on Finance. Perhaps Long, the son of Huey Long, saw an opportunity to extend his family's populist tradition. At the time, his committee was shaping what would become the Employee Retirement Income Security Act of 1974. Long used that act as a vehicle to move ESOPs from theory to reality. The act recognized ESOPs as qualified employee benefit plans, and exempted them from the prohibition against leveraging generally applicable to such plans.

The subsequent growth in the number of ESOPs is difficult to trace because Department of Labor (DOL) data do not unambiguously identify them. Some estimates include similar non-ESOP stock bonus plans (and perhaps other types of plans as well) in their counts of ESOPs. Nevertheless, the number of ESOPs apparently peaked in the mid-1980s (rising to about 11,000 by 1986), and then stabilized at about 8,000 by 1990 (see Conte and Jampani, 1996). The National Center for Employee Ownership (1996b) has estimated that 9,500 ESOPs and stock bonus plans existed in 1996, based on a projection of 1992 DOL data.

At the request of Senator Long, the U.S. General Accounting Office (GAO) in 1984 started an evaluation to establish some basic facts about the reality that the ESOP vision had become. The research challenges and findings are interesting in themselves. The evaluation also illustrates, however, the potential of tax data as a powerful evaluation resource. In this case, tax data provided sophisticated measures of firm performance and supported a strong quasi-experimental design incorporating a short time series and non-equivalent control group. Because direct access to federal tax data is not available to most researchers and IRS summaries may not suffice for particular research purposes, evaluators may benefit from some reflection on the advantages and disadvantages of using tax data before pursuing them. A second, more generally applicable lesson is that evaluators should recognize cost comparisons as information that can powerfully influence decision makers. The GAO's study (1986, 1987), for example, helped persuade Congress to eliminate the tax credit for certain ESOPs.

What are Employee Stock Ownership Plans?

Employee stock ownership plans are qualified employee benefit plans, recognized under the Employee Retirement Income Security Act of 1974 and later legislation. Their distinctive feature as pension plans is that ESOPs are designed to make employees stockholders in the firms that employ them. Under an ESOP plan, the corporation contributes its stock, or assets to buy its stock, into an ESOP trust that maintains tax-deferred individual accounts for participating employees. Unlike most other types of pension plans, ESOPs must be invested primarily in the securities of the sponsoring employer rather than in a diversified portfolio.

ESOPs can be considered as a tax expenditure program. They provide tax incentives for corporations that sponsor them. For its contributions to the ESOP, the corporation receives a tax deduction (or tax credits for certain types of ESOPs before 1987). In addition, employees participating in ESOPs pay no taxes on the amounts contributed to their accounts or on the earnings generated by funds in their accounts until they receive those funds. (Other tax incentives, such as to lenders, also have been added or terminated over the years.) ESOP tax incentives resulted in federal revenue losses of between $12.1 and $13.3 billion during the period of 1977–83 (see U.S. General Accounting Office, 1986, ch. 3).

Two tax incentives are of particular interest. First, the leveraging provisions allow—but do not require—the sponsoring corporation to arrange a tax-favored loan through the ESOP. It works like this. The corporation establishes an ESOP trust on behalf of the employees. The trust then borrows from a financial institution to purchase shares in the sponsoring corporation. The firm subsequently makes contributions to the trust sufficient to meet principal and interest payments on the loan. Because these payments are made to an employee benefit plan, they are fully tax deductible. In effect the corporation is able to deduct from pre-tax income both principal and interest payments on the ESOP loan, whereas only interest payments on business loans are ordinarily tax deductible. In theory, at least, this could provide a powerful incentive for firms to finance capital formation through ESOPs, rather than conventional loans, resulting in both economic growth and increased stock ownership on the part of employees, as envisioned by Kelso.

Second, some ESOPs were eligible for tax credits. Initially this was an add-on to the investment tax credit, but because that approach favored capital-intensive over labor-intensive industries, the basis was soon changed to payroll expenses. A company sponsoring this type of ESOP could contribute shares of its own stock (or cash to buy such shares) to the ESOP trust, up to an amount equal to 0.5 percent of the total payroll costs of covered employees. Remarkably, the tax credit provided was equal to the value of this contribution on a dollar-for-dollar basis. In other words, the Treasury subsidized this employee benefit in full, a unique incentive.

What are the Central Issues in Evaluating Employee Stock Ownership Plans?

The specified purpose of ESOP legislation was broadening the ownership of stock by transferring stock ownership to employees, and providing a means of raising capital through leveraged ESOPs. Although not specified in legislation, some advocates of ESOPs also view them as a way to improve the economic performance of sponsoring firms or to expand employees' influence over the management of their firms of employment. To the extent that ESOPs could deliver on this goal of improving corporate performance, federal tax revenue losses associated with ESOPs might be justified as a way to raise the national standard of living or to compete better internationally.

In 1984 Senator Long requested that the GAO (1986, 1987) conduct a study to: (1) provide an accurate count of ESOPs; (2) identify the factors associated with a company's decision to establish and continue an ESOP; (3) estimate the cost of ESOPs in lost federal tax revenues; (4) measure the degree to which ESOPs were expanding the ownership of capital; and (5) determine the relationship between a firm's sponsorship of an ESOP and improvements in its productivity and profitability.

Although this chapter focuses on the last of these objectives, each of the others also presented its own methodological challenges. To count ESOPs (objective 1), the GAO conducted a survey of a stratified sample of 2,004 plans among the 8,891 plans the Internal Revenue Service (IRS) had identified as possible ESOPs, based on filing information for 1979–83. A survey was necessary because the IRS data only indicated that these plans were reported to have "ESOP features," and the GAO needed to determine which plans actually met the legal definition of an ESOP. Combining survey responses with other data from IRS data files allowed reporting on a variety of aspects of the plan as well as their numbers. To identify company reasons for establishing and continuing ESOPs (objective 2) as well as additional firm and ESOP characteristics, the GAO conducted a second survey of those companies determined actually to have ESOPs. To estimate the cost of ESOPs in lost federal tax revenue (objective 3), the GAO used IRS data on annual contributions to, earnings of, and distributions from ESOP trusts. Varying assumptions and estimating procedures produced a range of estimates of tax costs. To measure the degree to which ESOPs were expanding the ownership of capital (objective 4), the evaluation combined survey results with IRS data to chart the growth of ESOP assets and participants over time.

Research Design for the Impact Analysis. One tradition in program evaluation is to judge an impact design relative to its vulnerability to threats to internal validity, that is, threats to the measured impact (in this case corporate performance) being due to factors other than the treatment (here, adopting an ESOP). The gold standard in this tradition is the experimental design, characterized by random assignment of cases to treatment and comparison groups in order to ensure that later measured differences between the groups can be attributed to the treatment, rather than being biased by initial systematic differences between the groups. Such a design was not feasible in this case, because the GAO could not control firms' decisions to sponsor, or not to sponsor, ESOPs. Instead, the approach chosen was a variation on a non-equivalent control group design, a quasi-experimental design that has been recommended when true experimental designs are not possible (see Campbell and Stanley, 1966, pp. 47–50; see also Boruch, 1997).

A first aspect of the design was a short time series of the performance of ESOP firms, calling for data for the two years before the ESOP was formed, the year it was formed, and the three years following formation, a total of six years. The design thus allowed a comparison of the performance of ESOP firms in the years immediately before they established their ESOPs to the years after.

The second aspect of the design was a short time series of the performance of a matched set of non-ESOP firms, which served as a non-equivalent control group. One problem with solely comparing performance before and after the formation of the ESOP is that any changes might reflect factors not associated with the formation of the ESOP at all. For example, if the ESOP firms showed some increase in productivity after plan formation, this might be attributable to the ESOP, but also might reflect general economic trends, random variation, or other factors. To determine whether non-ESOP factors accounted for any observed changes in ESOP firm performance, a sample of firms without ESOPs was selected to represent the trends in profitability and productivity for similar firms over the years studied. This non-ESOP comparison group was made as similar to the ESOP sample as possible by matching the two sets of firms by industry and size based on IRS data.

A secondary line of analysis concerning performance examined whether eight factors were associated with performance among the ESOP firms. The factors were derived from the first survey of ESOPs (for factors such as type of ESOP), the second more detailed survey of ESOP characteristics (for factors such as degree of employee influence on corporate decision making), and tax data for the same firms (for industry and firm size). The productivity and performance measures were derived from the tax data and based on the profitability and productivity measures used in the analysis of impact. The design was correlational—a regression analysis of the eight factors with measures of the proportional changes in profitability and profitability for each firm after it sponsored an ESOP.

Measures of Performance. Firm performance, a complex concept, was measured in two ways—profitability and productivity—in the hope of better capturing its various dimensions. Productivity is a major factor influencing profits, but because other factors (such as planning and development, marketing and selling, and financing) also strongly affect profits, profitability trends may diverge from productivity trends. Thus, these measures together give a fuller picture of firm performance than either can do singly. Also, because each of the measures has its strengths and weaknesses, using two measures provides more confidence in our findings if they converge for both measures.

Although profitability can be measured in a number of ways, the GAO's access to financial data from corporate tax returns allowed measuring profitability as after-tax return on assets. After-tax return on assets reflects the efficiency with which a corporation uses its assets. In order to ensure a fairer comparison between firms that raise funds in different ways, the measure was adjusted to compensate for the different tax effects on profits from raising corporate funds through loans or stock offerings.

The market value of assets would be the preferred measure of assets for analysis. However, tax returns provide information only on the historical value of such assets as buildings and other depreciable assets. Although older fixed capital may be undervalued by using this indicator, it was the best measure available.

Productivity was defined as labor productivity, measured as the ratio of real value added to real labor compensation. Productivity measures in general indicate the efficiency with which production inputs are used to create production outputs. Any measure of labor productivity expresses this relationship as one between some measure of output, such as the dollar value of output or the number of units produced, and some measure of labor input, such as hours paid or number of employees. A measure of labor productivity was constructed from the financial data on corporate tax returns. Output was measured as a form of value added (the value of output after adjusting for inventories and costs of materials), and labor input as total labor compensation (salaries, wages, and benefits). Because both labor compensation and value added were deflated by industry specific deflators, the measure is the ratio of real value added to real unit of labor input.

The productivity measure rested on several assumptions. Because the measure of labor input as labor costs can reflect movements in either the price or quantity of labor, it is assumed that changes in price after deflation reflect the quality and quantity of labor input. Second, we are assuming that our industry wide deflators accurately deflate labor costs for the matched firms. (Because the concern is with relative differences in productivity between ESOP and non-ESOP firms, different rates of compensation growth are more of a problem for bias than constant differences in compensation, even over long periods of time.) The third assumption is that sponsoring an ESOP does not change the level or growth of compensation relative to similar non-ESOP firms. For instance, the measure of productivity would be biased against ESOP firms if they raised wages faster than other firms due to their tax advantages.

To lessen the chance of a biased comparison between firms, the productivity measure was adjusted to be less sensitive to different timing of compensation changes. Firms may differ somewhat in the timing of compensation changes, but assuming that compensation rates for firms within an industry tend to equalize over time, the average compensation over several years will show less divergence than the trends for those years. Consequently, productivity was averaged both for the pre-ESOP period and the post-ESOP period. Although the productivity measure had some shortcomings, it was the closest approximation to a physical measure of productivity that could be derived given data constraints.

Sample. The primary estimate of impact came from comparing a sample of firms with ESOPs that had established their plans during the period 1976 through 1979 with a sample of matched non-ESOP firms. The earlier survey to count the number of ESOPs identified a national sample of approximately 1,100 ESOP firms. From this national sample of ESOPs, all those 414 firms that established an ESOP in their 1976–79 tax periods were selected. 1979 was the latest year of ESOP formation permitting examination of three years of performance after the ESOP was formed because more recent returns might be unavailable due to IRS processing.

Those firms that adopted ESOPs in their 1976–79 tax periods were matched to non-ESOP firms by industry and firm size. The IRS performed the matching, using a 1977 sample of about 90,600 corporations. The match was made precisely on an industry code and then to the closest size, as measured by revenue in the 1977 tax period, the earliest tax year for which data were readily available.

The match on Principal Business Activity (PBA), which is the Internal Revenue Service's classification of industry, was exact on a four digit code, but may include some error that would affect the adequacy of our matching. The error might arise from the corporate taxpayer entering the wrong PBA code, or the code being an oversimplification of the business interests of a firm with multiple lines of business activity.

Although potentially serious, these problems were not considered particularly worrisome for this analysis. Some inaccuracy in matching might have been introduced, but there was no reason to think that the bias would systematically favor the ESOP or non-ESOP firms. Moreover, errors in matching would only have a markedly adverse effect on the comparison of matched pairs if the misclassifications were severe. However, there was no reason to believe that the taxpayers grossly miscoded the PBAs on the returns. Finally, among firms in the sample with the needed six tax returns, 63 percent did not file consolidated returns for an affiliated group of corporations. Consolidated returns are probably our best indicator of possible diversification—although the affiliated corporations may be integrated into the same industry—so the problem of different patterns of diversification does not appear to be a serious one here.

The match on firm size as measured by receipts provided an accurate matching. At the median, the non-ESOP firm almost exactly matched the size of the paired ESOP firm (that is, it had revenues equal to those of the ESOP firm). Moreover, a large percentage of the non-ESOP firms were closely matched to their paired ESOP firms. For instance, 75 percent of the non-ESOPs in the productivity sample had revenues that were no more than 3.1 percent above or 5.2 percent below those of their matched ESOP firms.

Some survival bias might exist in the comparison of ESOP and non-ESOP firms resulting from sampling procedures. ESOP firms that had not survived to respond to the 1985 survey were not included in the sample. In contrast, the non-ESOP firms remained in our sample if they survived through a tax period during 1979–82, depending on which was the last tax period we examined. Thus, the sample of ESOP firms may have had a disproportionate share of poorer performing firms screened out, which could potentially lead to overestimating the effect of ESOPs. However, any non-ESOP firm for which the last examined return was the final return filed for the corporation was dropped from the sample. Moreover, one analysis, discussed later, statistically matches the performance of the ESOP and non-ESOP samples for the pre-ESOP period, which serves to lessen the impact of any survival bias on the estimated ESOP effect.

Data Collection. The financial data used to measure profitability and productivity in both the ESOP and non-ESOP samples came from the corporate income tax returns filed by those firms, copies of which were supplied by the Internal Revenue Service (IRS). Data were collected on each firm for a six-year period. The precise years used depended on the year of formation of the ESOP for each pair of firms (one with an ESOP and a matching firm without), with the earliest data coming from 1974 (for ESOPs formed in 1976) and the latest from 1982 (for ESOPs established in 1979). Additional data came from two surveys of the ESOP sample conducted in 1985, and from computer data on employee plans provided by the IRS.

The initial sample consisted of 414 ESOP and matched non-ESOP firms, but the usable sample was much smaller, largely due to the data burden inherent in the design and problems of data collection. Cases were excluded from this group if (1) the firms were not active throughout the required six-year period, (2) they did not file tax returns for each of the covered years, or (3) it was impossible to recover tax returns for both the ESOP and matched non-ESOP firms for the needed tax years. In addition, cases were excluded if the approximately fifty needed data items could not extracted from the return. As a result, the usable sample became 111 sets of firms, although not all of these could be used for all analyses.

Although the sample of ESOP firms was reduced from 414 to 111 usable for analysis, no major bias was detected in the sample. The composition of the sample approximated the distribution of all ESOPs on such dimensions as industry, type of ownership, and type of ESOP. Nevertheless, given the multiple stages in sampling and the reduction of our sample, claims were not made about the generalizability of estimates.

Analysis of Impact. Two different statistical procedures were used to test for a statistically significant association between ESOPs and improved corporate performance. If these two lines of analysis employing different statistical strategies reached congruent findings, confidence in the findings would be strengthened.

The first procedure, analysis of covariance (ANCOVA), allowed estimation of the change in performance associated with sponsoring an ESOP and testing whether this change is likely a chance occurrence due to the make-up of the sample of firms. ANCOVA statistically equalizes the profitability of the ESOP and non-ESOP firms in the pre-ESOP period, and then estimates how different the predicted profit rates for the ESOP and non-ESOP firms would be after ESOP sponsorship.

The second procedure, multivariate analysis of variance (MANOVA), employs a different strategy for identifying a profitability improvement among the ESOP firms. MANOVA's strength is an ability to test for differential trends between the matched pairs of ESOP and non-ESOP firms. MANOVA was used to tested for three patterns that would reasonably indicate performance improvement related to ESOPs. One reasonable pattern would show ESOP firms' profitability or productivity growing faster than matched non-ESOP firms after adopting the ESOPs. A second pattern would show ESOP firms jumping to a clearly higher profitability level relative to the non-ESOP firms the year after sponsoring an ESOP. A third pattern is identical to the second, except the jump occurs after a lag, in the second year after sponsoring an ESOP.

Findings. No consistent and statistically significant profitability or productivity improvements were associated with sponsoring an ESOP. As shown in Table 4.1, the ANCOVA analyses generally did not confirm profitability improvements. Only the estimate for firms sponsoring ESOPs in 1976–77, indicating a 2.7 percent profitability improvement during the second year, was statistically significant at the .05 level. This improvement appeared transitory, if not spurious; the estimate for the third year is positive but not statistically significant. Moreover, estimates for the firms sponsoring ESOPs in 1978–79 were all negative, though not statistically significant. As with the ANCOVA analysis, the MANOVA analysis did not substantiate a profitability trend associated with sponsoring an ESOP. None of the tested patterns reasonably associated with profitability improvement were statistically significant.

Findings were similar for the analyses of productivity, as shown in Table 4.2. ANCOVA estimates were negative but not statistically significant. In other words, the productivity differences were not large enough relative to the variation in productivity in the sample of ESOP and non-ESOP firms to reject the possibility that ESOP firms perform as well as similar non-ESOP firms. MANOVA also did not substantiate a productivity trend associated with sponsoring an ESOP.

Analysis of the relationships between changes in corporate performance before and after establishment of an ESOP and eight factors that have been proposed as likely contributors to corporate success in ESOP firms resulted in only one statistically significant finding: the greater the degree of employee participation in corporate decision making, the higher the rate of change in

Table 4.1. ANCOVA Estimates of ESOP Effect on Profitability

Firms with ESOPS	Year after Sponsoring	Percent Change	Confidence Interval	Significant at .05 Level	N of Pairs
ESOPs formed in 1976–77	First	–2.0%	±4.2%	No	63
	Second	2.7%	±2.6%	Yes	63
	Third	3.4%	±5.2%	No	63
ESOPs formed in 1978–79	First	–1.1%	±4.6%	No	43
	Second	–3.4%	±6.1%	No	43
	Third	–3.7%	±8.2%	No	43

Source: U.S. General Accounting Office, 1987, p. 17.

Table 4.2. ANCOVA Estimates of ESOP Effect on Productivity

Firms with ESOPS	Year after Sponsoring	Percent Change	Confidence Interval	Significant at .05 Level	N of Pairs
ESOPs formed in 1976–77	First	−3.5%	±14.1%	No	25
ESOPS formed in 1978–79	First	−5.4%	±23.8%	No	20

Source: U.S. General Accounting Office, 1987, p. 24.

the measure of productivity between the pre-ESOP and post-ESOP periods. No other variable examined was significantly related to changes in either profitability or the productivity measure.

Conclusions and Reflections. The evaluation did not substantiate assertions that ESOPs improve either profitability or productivity. Several caveats were noted. Given the relatively large confidence intervals around the estimates, the sample of firms may have been too small to reliably detect improvements, particularly for productivity effects. Also, the productivity indicator may still have had sufficient bias to obscure an ESOP effect despite efforts to lessen distortions. Finally, the measurements for the three years after the sponsorship of an ESOP may not have been long enough for the effect to appear.

In various literature summaries, this finding has probably been characterized in all logically possible ways. It has been dismissed on the grounds of some research weakness, portrayed as part of the inconclusive evidence about ESOPs' impact, seen as supporting the lack of evidence that ESOPs harm performance, or essentially ignored in statements that some studies have found ESOPs correlated with improved performance. (See Blasi, 1990; National Center for Employee Ownership, 1996a.)

The value of the impact conclusions should not be judged in isolation but rather in the context of the overall project. The impact analysis was part of a broader picture about ESOPs being drawn for Congress. The broader project had described the number of ESOPs, costs of ESOP incentives, the value of stock transferred through ESOPs, and the frequency of using leveraged loans. From a federal policy perspective, a key issue was, for example, whether the cost of ESOP incentives was offset by increased taxes due to increased profitability. Being able to say that such an offset could not be substantiated was an important part of the picture. Not addressing this issue would have resulted in a less balanced picture.

Also, the impact findings served an important purpose by bringing additional findings to an ongoing debate in the literature on ESOPs. Perhaps the most legitimate effect of the study was to sound a note of caution against those arguing that previous studies were strong enough to assert a positive impact. The GAO review of the literature concluded that prior studies were inconclusive on this question, because of both mixed results and research weaknesses (U.S. General Accounting Office, 1987, appendix I). Moreover, the mixed and inconclusive findings in the literature are probably to be expected when fairly small differences in performance (say 1 to 3 percent) are substantively important, and (as noted by Conte and Svejnar, 1990, p. 171) estimated effects appear very dependent on research design and equation specifications. From the perspective of later meta-analyses, we were contributing a fairly strong evaluation with findings to be compared with those of other research.

Were There Lessons for Future Evaluations?

First, the evaluation revealed that tax data can provide powerful support for evaluations. At the same time it highlighted some of the disadvantages and advantages of using corporate tax returns as a data source. These considerations may be helpful when contemplating the use of tax data in future evaluations. Second, the project suggests comparative cost information can strongly influence decisions about a program's fate. For the GAO project, tax returns provided the necessary information.

Disadvantages of Tax Data. The real stumbling block to the use of federal tax data is access. Access is restricted by law and regulation. Thus direct access to tax data is not possible for most researchers.

A second disadvantage is that tax data have the typical problems of secondary data. The data are designed to serve the IRS's purposes of tax collection, and may less well serve particular research purposes. For example, as noted above, it would have been easier if some corporate data had not been rolled up in consolidated returns and if the IRS had collected data on number of employees, total hours worked, physical outputs, market value of assets, and other factors.

Extracting tax data from returns is time consuming. In part, difficulty arose because data were needed from a variety of schedules rather than just from the main tax form 1120. The schedules must be located, and even then the needed entries may not be there, but rather on some taxpayer-created attachment. Moreover, level of detail is not consistently entered by all firms, and entire industries, such as utilities, may have unique accounting entries driven by such factors as regulatory reporting requirements; such differences require additional time to ensure uniform extraction. And the sheer volume of a consolidated return for many corporations, a return that might fill a large box, makes finding the data for a single firm an even lengthier task.

To save extraction time, limit data collection to items on the main tax form and on as few schedules as possible. Hopefully, increased electronic submission of tax data will allow electronic extraction rather than examination of physical documents. Electronic extraction may well ease the burden of data collection (and make recent data available more quickly). It is uncertain whether electronic extraction will make it more difficult to separate data for firms in consolidated returns or find missing data in taxpayer attachments. The price of easier extraction could be less available information.

Finally, the most recent returns may not be readily available because of IRS processing. For this reason, for data collection starting in 1985, returns were not requested for any later than 1982. Because ESOP legislation had been in place for about a decade when the study began, this limitation was not a severe one for this evaluation. However, the loss of the most recent years could be very problematic for some studies.

Advantages of Using Tax Data. The above discussion reads as faint praise for tax data as a data source. However, the value of tax returns as a data source should be judged in comparison with the other available options. As Conte and Svejnar (1990, p. 164) noted in their review of the literature, the GAO's "data base was perhaps the best yet available to study the performance effects of ESOPs." Some other studies had relied on publicly available financial information on firms, which effectively excludes the majority of ESOP-sponsoring firms because most are privately held. Alternatively, other studies had gathered data from the voluntary reporting of firms; these requests for financial data frequently led to high non-response rates and thus to a suspicion of a self-selection bias in the responses.

The comparative advantages of tax data are several. Tax data can provide a rich source of financial data about firms cross-sectionally and over time. Data were potentially available from essentially the universe of viable firms. Because submission of the data is generally compulsory for firms, bias from self-selection is negligible. Also, using tax data poses no additional burden on corporate respondents, who are often inundated by data requests and may have blanket policies of nonresponse. Finally, electronic processing might increase evaluator access if tight privacy screens are applied and legal barriers are overcome.

The Value of Information on Comparative Costs. Comparative-cost data related to important program outcomes can be powerful information for decision-makers. Whether through tax data or some other sources, researchers should consider providing such information.

The most influential of the findings derived from a cost comparison between two types of ESOPs, one of which received tax deductions and the other tax credits. The tax-credit ESOPs accounted for 89 to 97 percent of foregone federal tax revenue, but the value of assets in such ESOPs was only $1.25 for each dollar of lost revenue. This fairly high cost resulted largely from the dollar-to-dollar credit for contributions to tax credit ESOPs. In contrast, the tax-deduction type of ESOP added an estimated $2.56 to $16.99 of assets to participants' accounts for every dollar of revenue lost. Moreover, the tax credit ESOP provided less in assets per participant than did the tax-deduction ESOP. These findings were influential in Congress's decision to terminate tax credits for ESOPs in the 1986 Tax Reform Act.

It is worth speculating about why this relatively simple cost comparison was so influential. First, a more rigorous design was not necessary because causality was not assumed to be a complex issue. It was not critical to demonstrate that federal incentives had caused the ESOP trusts to increase, or what corporate behavior would have been in the absence of tax credit ESOP incentives. Second, the contrast of costs and outcomes was striking. Compared to tax-deduction ESOPs, tax-credit ESOPs accounted for almost all of the costs but provided quite little above these costs in the ESOP accounts. Third, the finding compared the relative costs of parts of the program (tax-credit versus tax-deduction incentives) and associated outcomes relative to a major goal of the program's outcome, that is, the transfer of stock ownership. Fourth, costs were important to decision makers; concerns over federal deficit reduction had heightened sensitivity to costs.

Social scientists have heard the criticism that their work does no more than reveal their keen sense for the obvious. In this case, after all, tax credit provisions meant the government subsidized the transfer of stock at a 100 percent rate, within certain limits. To know this was a generous subsidy, one needed to research no further than the tax code. However, the results put numbers to the costs and outcomes and gave realism to this obvious fact about the tax code. The lesson is that the obvious may need detailed facts to make it salient and understandable.

References

Blasi, J. R. "Comment [on 'The Performance Effects of Employee Ownership Plans']." In A. Blinder (ed.), *Paying for Productivity: A Look at the Evidence*. Washington, D.C.: The Brookings Institution, 1990.

Boruch, R. F. *Randomized Controlled Experiments for Planning and Evaluation*. Thousand Oaks, Calif.: Sage, 1997.

Campbell, D. T., and Stanley, J. C. *Experimental and Quasi-Experimental Designs for Research*. Chicago: Rand McNally, 1966.

Conte, M. A., and Svejnar, J. "The Performance Effects of Employee Ownership Plans." In A. Blinder (ed.), *Paying for Productivity: A Look at the Evidence*. Washington, D.C.: The Brookings Institution, 1990.

Conte, M. A., and Jampani, R. "Financial Returns of ESOPs and Similar Plans." In P. A. Fernandez, J. A. Turner, and R. P. Hinz (eds.), *Pensions, Savings, and Capital Markets*. Washington, D.C.: U.S. Department of Labor, 1996.

Kelso, L. O., and Adler, M. *The Capitalist Manifesto*. New York: Random House, 1958.

National Center for Employee Ownership. "Employee Ownership and Corporate Performance." http://www.nceo.org, Oakland, Calif.: National Center for Employee Ownership, 1996a.

National Center for Employee Ownership. "A Statistical Profile of Employee Ownership." http://www.nceo.org, Oakland, Calif.: National Center for Employee Ownership, 1996b.

U.S. General Accounting Office. *Employee Stock Ownership Plans: Benefits and Costs of ESOP Tax Incentives for Broadening Stock Ownership*. Washington, D.C.: U.S. General Accounting Office, 1986.

U.S. General Accounting Office. *Employee Stock Ownership Plans: Little Evidence of Effects on Corporate Performance*. Washington, D.C.: U.S. General Accounting Office, 1987.

TERRY J. HANFORD is a senior evaluator and core group leader at the U.S. General Accounting Office, Denver, Colorado.

*Enterprise zones are intended to revitalize America's economically
distressed cities and rural areas, relying primarily on tax and
regulatory relief to encourage private investment in areas that
otherwise might be unattractive. Congress requested a prospective
evaluation based on a state program with similar features. The
evaluation used multiple methods and data sources both to enrich
findings and to protect against unwarranted conclusions.*

Use of Quasi-Experimental Methods in Tax Expenditure Evaluation: The Case of Maryland Enterprise Zones

Scott Crosse, Patrick G. Grasso, Monica Kelly

One of the enduring legacies of post–World War II America was the long-term
deterioration of central cities as millions of families in a growing middle class
fled to suburban communities pursuing the American Dream: a single-family
home, a verdant lawn, and top-flight public schools for the kids. Businesses
soon followed, leaving most older cities with a residuum of poor and lower-
middle-class residents, along with a shortage of jobs, an aging infrastructure,
and a lack of such amenities as decent schools, well-maintained parks, or even
basic public safety.

As a result, reversing the decline of older central cities has been the preoccupation of those concerned with urban public policy for nearly half a cen-
tury. Rural areas were not immune, either. Often dependent on one major
employer, many small communities began to find themselves in deep distress
as manufacturing jobs, in particular, were lost first to lower-cost regions of the
United States, and later to foreign sources of competition.

At least as early as the 1950s, the federal government initiated efforts to
help cities reverse this vicious downward spiral, or at least to alleviate its most
obvious effects. Urban renewal during the 1950s and 1960s generally proved
unsuccessful, often leaving behind the ugly scars of vacant lots, failed sky-
scrapers, and dangerous high-rise public housing projects. The Model Cities program developed during the Johnson Administration was supposed to
concentrate billions of dollars and a coordinated inter-agency effort into rebuild-
ing a small number of cities as a demonstration of what could be done to save
urban America; but congressional logrolling resulted in a program that dispersed

relatively small amounts of money to about 125 communities in all 50 states, ensuring that little actually could be accomplished (Grasso, 1986). In the 1970s Urban Development Action Grants and Community Development Block Grants supported downtown revitalization efforts in some cities, but conditions outside the central business districts often grew worse, and in any case the coming of the Reagan Administration signaled the end of those programs (Hanson, 1991). Such failures paved the way for a new approach beginning in the 1980s—enterprise zones.

What Are Enterprise Zones?

The enterprise zone (EZ) idea was developed in the United Kingdom in the late 1970s as an answer to the spread of "urban blight." Credit for the idea is contested, but most analysts cite the work of British urban planner Peter Hall (1981) as seminal. Hall did not propose EZs as a panacea for urban ills, but rather as an experiment to see if unbridled capitalism could trump the efforts of city planners. In an ironic twist, Sir Geoffrey Howe, later a leading member of the Thatcher Cabinet, picked up on some of Hall's ideas with a proposal that small enclaves should be created in the most depressed areas of British cities in which virtually all taxes and government regulations would be eliminated. These measures, he reasoned, would encourage private enterprise to flourish, and lead to a revival of those areas that no government-run program was likely to accomplish (Butler, 1991). Howe's ideas were carried to the United States by Stuart M. Butler, whose 1979 monograph on EZs for the Heritage Foundation was influential in getting the concept into the public policy debate (Butler, 1979).

Butler's work inspired Jack Kemp, then a Republican congressman from the Buffalo area, who saw EZs as a way to bring conservative ideas to the policy debates on urban decline. Rather than simply nay-saying, conservatives could rally around a positive program, one that relied on the forces of the market—rather than the command and control systems of the federal government—to attack the perplexing problems of inner city decay. Beginning in 1980, Kemp, later joined by Bronx Democrat Robert Garcia, led a crusade for passage of a federal enterprise zone program, a crusade he continued as Secretary of the Department of Housing and Urban Development (HUD) during the Bush Administration.

Despite Kemp's enthusiasm, legislative action came slowly. Congress passed legislation in 1987 permitting HUD to identify up to 100 EZs, but that act provided no specific benefits for the zones, making it essentially symbolic. In fact, a national EZ program was not enacted until 1993; that program, a Clinton Administration initiative, differed sharply from the Kemp–Garcia proposal. Despite the lack of action in Congress, however, nearly 40 states had initiated their own EZ efforts by the late 1980s, partly in anticipation of eventual passage of federal legislation. These state enterprise zone programs vary widely in terms of eligibility criteria, tax and other benefits, and administration. Most, however, share certain common characteristics: the zones are geographically defined areas; participating businesses are eligible for certain tax incentives, usually tied to job creation and investment in plant and equipment; and there are additional benefits for hiring the unemployed or welfare recipients.

In Britain, EZs were established largely to develop vacant areas of cities, with expected spillover benefits to surrounding neighborhoods a secondary concern. The primary objective was to put idle space into productive use. By contrast, in the United States the aim has been to use EZs to revitalize neighborhoods and to provide jobs for the unemployed and the poor. This difference in focus meant that the kinds of firms sought for EZs also was different. If the goal is to fill vacant space, the most likely target would be large companies with the wherewithal to invest in major new construction. But if the program is designed to produce jobs for local people, then small businesses, which can fit into existing structures, make a more sensible target (Butler, 1991).

In the United States, therefore, the tax incentives for EZs are designed to address small business's needs. For such companies, the major concerns are the need for capital and the costs of labor. Not surprisingly, most EZ programs include incentives for investment and tax credits tied to employment, especially of residents in or near the zones (Butler, 1991). These incentives may be especially important because the costs of doing business in the zones, and especially of providing employment to workers living in the zone areas, may be unusually higher. Enterprise zones tend to be in areas where the physical infrastructure is poor and security risks high, problems that mean higher costs for transportation, utilities, insurance, and security. And many of the low-income workers the zones are expected to help find employment lack the job skills and work habits that make them attractive to employers.

What Are the Central Issues in Evaluating Enterprise Zones?

The evaluation reported here was conducted by the U.S. General Accounting Office (GAO) in response to a 1986 request from then-Congressmen Kemp and Garcia (U.S. General Accounting Office, 1988). The major evaluation issue concerned the ability of EZs to deliver—that is, actually to produce economic benefits for the designated communities. In practice, this hinged on the extent to which new jobs could be created in the EZs.

A second issue concerned the net costs of EZs. Supporters of a national EZ program argued that the secondary benefits of EZs would more than pay for the costs of the tax expenditures to support them. For example, they claimed that many people then receiving welfare or other social benefits would find employment in the zones, thus reducing expenditures for social programs and, indeed, turning the recipients into taxpayers themselves. In short, EZs not only could revive our declining urban and rural areas, but we could do it for nothing, or maybe even come out ahead—quite an economic miracle.

The optimistic religion of EZ supporters—mostly supply-side economists and their followers—was strongly challenged by the more tradition-bound grinches at the U.S. Treasury Department. (The Treasury method is described in Spilberg and Kern, 1982.) Their economic simulations indicated that the federal program could cost as much as $4.75 billion in net revenue losses just in the first six years of the program. Critical to this conclusion was Treasury's assumption that any business or employment increases generated in the EZs could occur only at the expense of other areas. Hence, rather than creating new employment opportunities, the federal program would incur costs to shift existing opportunities into the EZs. Under this scenario, the program would generate little or nothing in the way of cost offsets through reductions in social service demand or increased tax payments from former welfare recipients.

Of course, skepticism about EZs was not limited to Treasury analysts. Opponents argued that tax expenditures were an inefficient and probably ineffective method of promoting economic development compared to direct spending. They noted that tax breaks (other than for sales taxes) were of little use to most start-up companies, which frequently did not have tax liabilities in their difficult early years, but that larger companies could find them of use. This would tend to encourage firms such as retail chains to relocate into the zones, depriving nearby—often equally distressed—areas of businesses and jobs. Moreover, there was little evidence that the tax credits for hiring the disadvantaged could be effective, given the high costs of training workers (Levitan and Miller, 1992).

Thus, the debate between supply-siders and more traditional economists dictated the major evaluation issues: Did state-sponsored EZ programs actually increase employment within the areas where they applied? If so, to what extent did this lead to increased revenues and/or decreased social expenditures that could offset the revenue losses associated with the program?

What Were the Major Methodological Challenges Faced in the Study?

Three substantial methodological challenges surfaced: (1) developing a method to evaluate a prospective—rather than an ongoing—program; (2) designing a study that could determine whether any employment growth in EZs was attributable to the program; and (3) collecting data on geographical areas that corresponded to the EZs.

Evaluations of program effects typically are done on a post-hoc basis. But methods also have been developed to conduct prospective evaluations of programs not yet in place. One approach is the prospective evaluation synthesis (see U.S. General Accounting Office, 1990b), based on an analysis of evaluations of programs with features similar to those in the proposal. Unfortunately, that approach was not feasible here because at the time there was little literature on the effectiveness of enterprise zones. Thus, the study employed multiple methods, as described later in the chapter.

Assessing the extent to which changes would have occurred in the absence of an intervention is nearly always an issue in outcome or impact evaluations. In the case of EZs, the attribution issue was salient because state program administrators and EZ advocates often trumpeted the positive outcomes, particularly new jobs, "caused" by EZs, with little consideration for alternative explanations. But, following the recession of the early 1980s, the national economy experienced an expansion that almost certainly affected the areas in which the study's EZs were located. Hence, the challenge was to separate EZ-related changes (if any) from changes that would have occurred anyway as a result of improving general economic conditions. The best solution was an interrupted time-series analysis combined with a survey of enterprise zone employers.

Finally, collecting data on geographical areas that corresponded to the EZs was an especially vexing problem because EZs generally include only parts of the jurisdictions on which data are readily available. For example, the Bureau of Labor Statistics aggregates monthly data on employment levels by standard metropolitan areas or states. The 1980 decennial Census provided information on lower levels of aggregation (for example, census tracts), which was useful for the evaluation, but this information was not tracked for the years between censuses. As described in a later section, here the solution was developing our own sampling frames, taking advantage of the fact that EZs are geographically defined, so that firms located in those areas could be identified and incorporated into the study.

What Design Was Used?

To address these issues, the design embedded a quasi-experiment within a case study approach. The case studies paid particular attention to process issues—how the zones were administered and how employers reacted to program incentives. At the same time, the study used both quantitative and qualitative data to reach its conclusions. This combination of design elements makes the study unusual, certainly among tax expenditure evaluations. As it turned out, the selection of this multimethod design was crucial: it gave protection against a serious misinterpretation of the findings.

Case Studies. Case studies can provide a test of program effects and insights into the reasons for success or failure (see Yin, 1989; U.S. General Accounting Office, 1990a). To use case studies this way requires that the sites selected cannot represent widely diverse programs; there must be some underlying similarities in the cases so that reasonable inferences can be drawn (U.S. General Accounting Office, 1990a, pp.45–49). Moreover, the number of cases needs to be manageable to maintain the integrity of the in-depth data collection and analysis that are the strengths of the method. To meet these conditions and provide a fair test of the prospective federal program, it seemed best to conduct case studies of selected zones in a state whose EZ program was similar to the proposed federal program. Of course, the results of such a design are generalizable only to situations in which similar implementation conditions apply, rather than to all situations.

The study began with a review of the features of the state enterprise zone programs, comparing them to the Kemp–Garcia bill. The Maryland program was selected because it both matched many of the bill's features relatively closely and had been operating long enough to provide time for development effects to appear. Among similar features, both programs offered both a general tax credit for hiring, and additional credits for hiring disadvantaged workers, although the state program offered a lower level of benefits. In addition, they both offered tax incentives for investment in physical plant. The programs also shared many of the same eligibility criteria, including location in areas with high unemployment, poverty, and low-income household rates, or suffering severe population losses. (Details of the Maryland program are discussed below.)

Next, three case study sites within Maryland were selected. In selecting these best-case EZs, the evaluators considered the nominations of a state program official, and also reviewed program records on the performance of EZs, including information on the number of businesses that participated in the program and the number of employment opportunities that the local EZ administrators had claimed were created by their EZs. In the end, sites in Hagerstown, Salisbury and Cumberland were chosen as case sites, out of 13 EZs state-wide. Data also were collected on the Baltimore EZ, but it had not been in operation long enough to provide meaningful impact measures by the time of the study, so it was not selected as a study site.

Time-Series Design. Interrupted time-series (ITS) analyses were computed for each of the sample EZs (McCleary and Hay, 1980; Cook and Campbell, 1979). This quasi-experimental design provides a relatively strong test of program effects, where it can be used appropriately. Using ITS analysis requires a long series of data on the outcome variable of interest, in this instance data on employment in the Maryland zones. These data were analyzed by testing them against a series of autoregressive integrated moving average (ARIMA) models. Such models are designed to estimate the statistical effects of an intervention (for this study, implementation of an EZ) on the pattern of specific outcomes (change in total employment in the EZ) over a relatively long period of time (here, 90 months). ITS models were used to detect changes in either the rate of growth in employment (a change in the slope of the trend) or the level of employment.

To give the program a good chance to show effects, the ITS analysis began by examining employment trends only among the employers that actually participated in the EZ program. It is logical that if employers were adding to their work forces they would want to participate in the program and reap the tax benefits. If there were any program effects, they would show up among this group. The analysis would be extended to include non-participating employers located in the EZs only if initial effects were found among this "best-bet" group.

Before deciding on this design, several alternatives were considered. As in many practical evaluation situations, an experimental design was not feasible.

The GAO could not create an experimental EZ program, nor was it in a position to persuade a state to participate in such an experiment. Another design was a pretest-posttest study with a matched comparison group. That is, areas of other cities similar to the EZs could have been selected, employment over a time period extending before and after the EZs were implemented tracked, and comparisons of employment changes made. However, this design would have been much weaker in terms meeting the threats to valid causal inferences than ITS analysis (Cook and Campbell, 1979). Once it became apparent that the data requirements for the ITS analysis could be met, this clearly was the best choice.

Employer Survey. Other data came from examination of zone records and a survey of the EZ businesses, including both those participating in the EZ program and those not doing so. This feature of the study was intended to shed light on how local EZ programs operated, from the perspective of businesses located in the EZs. Information from this process-evaluation approach could be valuable for identifying program features that were especially important contributors to program success. Perhaps more important, however, this aspect of the evaluation offered the opportunity to bring additional evidence to bear on the results of the outcome analysis.

The plan was to examine the outcome results in conjunction with the process results: To the extent that the two analyses yielded a coherent pattern, more confidence could be placed in the findings. For example, if the ITS indicated program-related changes in employment in the zones, the process analysis could "rule in" the program intervention as the cause (for example, provide evidence that the intervention was sufficiently strong to produce the observed changes), and "rule out" alternative hypotheses (for example, evidence that the timing of other potential causal factors was inconsistent with the observed changes). As described in a later section, it was possible to identify the firms that were responsible for apparent program-related changes that showed up in the ITS analysis, and directly verify with those businesses the extent to which their participation in an EZ influenced their location and hiring decisions.

Criticism of the Design. Following completion of the study, Maryland EZ officials attacked the study design described above. As reported, and implicitly supported, by Levitan (1992, p. 48), these officials argued that the results for the three selected sites could not be used to reach judgments about the program's overall success. For one thing, all three were in small cities, and so were not representative of the program across the state. Moreover, for one of the study sites (Salisbury) the largest single employer was dropped from the reported analyses.

There are a number of ways in which study cases can be selected. The researchers may select a representative sample of cases, "typical" (or average) cases, or best and worst examples, depending on the purposes of the study. The GAO specifically sought out best-case sites to give the program the best chance to show how well it could work. In this instance, "best case" means, first, that the state program included features similar to the proposed federal program so that their effects could be reasonably estimated; second, that the zones in the study sites had been effectively implemented, so that any failure to find an effect could not be attributed to incomplete or otherwise faulty implementation; and, third, that the program had been in place for sufficient time to permit program effects to appear, because economic development—particularly the effort to turn around local economies with serious problems—takes time.

Thus, the fact that the sample was not representative is not a particularly telling criticism. As noted above, the absence of the only large-city program, in Baltimore, reflected nothing more than the short duration of that program at the time of the study, which rendered it not yet ripe for evaluation.

As for the analysis of the Salisbury data, the largest employer in that EZ was indeed not represented in the statistical results included in the report. But, as an appendix the report explains, all firms participating in the Salisbury EZ were included in the initial analyses, which found no effect of the zone on employment. However, because one firm accounted for a substantial fraction of total zone employment, the analysts were concerned that any effects among the remaining firms could be masked. Removing that employer from the analysis did not affect the conclusions of the study: with the employer in or out of the ARIMA models there was no statistically significant effect on employment in the Salisbury EZ.

What Measures Were Used?

The main independent variable for the first phase of the outcome analysis was implementation of the local EZs. Modeling the potential effects of EZs required that the evaluators specify the timing and nature of the implementation. This implementation tended to be gradual, over the course of several months. In the analysis, the evaluators also specified alternative implementation patterns (for example, abrupt implementation) for each of the three EZs. In each case, the date on which the EZ became fully operational was selected as the intervention point.

The major outcome of interest was employment in the zones. As discussed below, this was measured using state unemployment insurance (UI) records for employers located in each zone. To the extent that some employees may be exempt from the UI program or that employers do not accurately report all employees there is some underestimate of employment. However, neither of these was likely to be a major problem in the areas studied, and in any case such an undercount would not affect the trend in employment unless the rates of exemption or erroneous reporting also changed over time.

In addition to the primary outcome measure, it was necessary to estimate any cost offsets the zones might engender. The conceptual framework for the study posited that, to produce such offsets, EZs would first have to increase employment among the businesses located within EZ boundaries. This was a necessary but not sufficient step. To the extent that EZs did increase local employment, the evaluation would examine other links in the causal chain, including the extent to which: (a) increased employment included persons who had been receiving transfer payments, and (b) any such transfer payments were reduced as a result of the EZ-related employment. This would require information on the welfare status of new employees, including the amount of benefits received, and estimates of their tax payments to the state resulting from employment in the zones.

Other measures described aspects of program participation that potentially could confirm or disconfirm the results of the outcome analysis on employment levels. These measures included employer assessments of the importance for their recent location and hiring and investment decisions of: (a) various factors such as site characteristics, market access, and real estate costs; (b) features similar to those included in the Maryland and prospective federal EZ programs; and (c) various non-financial economic development incentives. Finally, the influence of EZ program participation, as perceived by firms, on specific location and hiring decisions was also assessed.

How Were the Data Collected and Analyzed?

As mentioned, a major challenge for the evaluation was collecting data on units that corresponded to the geographical areas encompassed by EZs and the solution was developing our own sampling frames for businesses located in two of the three EZs. (The plan was to survey program participants in all three EZs, and to survey all businesses in two of them.) Developing the sampling frames first required obtaining existing lists of businesses and evaluating the extent to which the lists covered the businesses located within the EZ boundaries. After inspecting the lists and visiting the EZs, it was clear that each list (which included lists developed by the local EZ administrators and local Chambers of Commerce, county property tax rolls, a directory of state manufacturers, and reverse telephone directories) was either outdated or missing a substantial number of businesses in the EZs for other reasons. Hence, the next step was to combine the lists, eliminate duplicate listings for businesses, check whether or not individual businesses on the combined lists were located within EZs, and revise the combined lists by systematically walking and driving around the EZs. While arduous, this effort was critical for the statistical analyses and provided qualitative information on the context in which the programs operated. The evaluators also asked the businesses in the mail survey to review a map of the EZ in their area and to confirm that they were located within the EZ boundaries.

Once confident that the sampling frames captured substantially all the businesses in the EZs, especially the firms with the most employees, the frames were used to gather data. For the outcome analysis, the evaluation used monthly data from the Maryland unemployment insurance system database. This database contains records on the mandated premiums paid by practically all commercial establishments in the state. It also contains monthly counts of employees for individual businesses over several years. Because the database used the same definitions and procedures during the period under consideration, it was appropriate for analyses over time. To use the database for the outcome analysis required extracting data for the companies participating in the program. In several cases, firms were called to confirm that the name in the database was for the same firm listed on the sampling frame.

Separate outcome analyses for each of the three EZs were run. Each outcome analysis required aggregating records on individual employers within the EZ over the course of 90 months (that is, April 1980 through September 1987). The ARIMA modeling followed an iterative process of identifying and testing alternative models until a model was developed for each EZ that met specified criteria (McCleary and Hay, 1980). As mentioned, the analysts tested models with different implementation patterns as well as models with and without the few largest employers, out of concern that data on these employers could overwhelm, statistically, measured effects for other businesses.

Final steps included reviewing the records of the local EZ programs, conducting a mail survey of businesses within the EZs, and interviewing representatives of specific businesses. The program records typically provided information on individual participants and claims for benefits. The mail survey, which was directed at all the businesses within a given EZ, collected information on the major process measures as well as on: (a) employer characteristics (for example, type of business); (b) experience with the Maryland EZ program; and (c) reasons for participating or not participating in the EZ program. In the wake of the outcome analysis, the officials in the businesses that appeared to be influenced by the EZ program were interviewed to explore further their motivation for relocating or increasing employment.

How Did the Maryland EZ Program Work?

Under the Maryland program, special tax and other incentives were available to areas designated as enterprise zones by state program administrators. To be designated at the time of the study, an area had to satisfy at least one of the following eligibility criteria:

- An unemployment rate in the area (or proximity) of at least 1.5 times the national or state level, whichever was higher
- Income of the population in the area (or proximity) below 125 percent of the national poverty level
- At least 70 percent of families in the area (or proximity) with incomes below 80 percent of the local median income, or
- A 10 percent or greater decrease in population in the area (or proximity) between the last two censuses, and either chronic property abandonment or substantial arrears in property tax payments

Designation as an enterprise zone was good for 10 years, but a maximum of only six could be selected during any twelve-month period, and no county could qualify for more than one EZ in any calendar year.

Once an area was designated, employers were eligible for a number of tax incentives. These included:

- A tax credit of up to $500 for each new job filled by a worker not previously laid off by the employer
- A three-year tax credit—worth up to $1,500 the first year, $1,000 the second, and $500 the third—for each new job filled by a disadvantaged worker not previously laid off by the employer
- A two-year tax credit—worth up to $1,000 the first year and $500 the second—for each rehired worker who had been laid off by the employer for at least six months, and
- A five-year tax credit against local property taxes equal to 80 percent of any increase in assessed value resulting from improvements, and another five years with a reduction of 10 percentage points each year

In addition to these tax incentives, the program included several other supports for EZs. The state would provide a 100 percent guarantee for long-term loans to finance fixed assets or working capital. It also would permit local governments to borrow more for industrial land acquisition, industrial park development, purchasing industrial sites, or building shell projects than normal; and make 25 percent more than the normal maximum available from the state industrial and commercial redevelopment fund.

What Were the Findings?

Initial analyses showed dramatically positive results. Two of the three sites—Hagerstown and Salisbury—experienced sizable employment increases among participating companies after the local EZs were implemented. (In Cumberland, there was no evidence to support EZ effects on employment.) The most striking results were found in Hagerstown. A city of 34,000 in the northwest part of the state, in the early 1980s Hagerstown suffered from many of the ills EZs are designed to counter: an unemployment rate of 14 percent, loss of a major employer, and substantial layoffs by another company. Soon after the state program was adopted, local officials sought EZ designation for a 2,000-acre area covering the old central business district, a large industrial park and several smaller industrial areas. The EZ was fully implemented by the end of December 1983.

Figure 5.1 shows the trend line for employment among companies participating in the Hagerstown EZ over the period studied; the vertical line represents the point at which implementation was complete. These companies increased the number of jobs by 16 percent during August and a stunning 19 percent in October of the same year. Not surprisingly, the ITS analysis confirmed that these changes in employment were statistically significant.

Ordinarily, the analysis would have ended here and the GAO might have concluded that the program did succeed in raising employment in the

Figure 5.1. Number of Employees for Participants in Hagerstown EZ, 1980–87

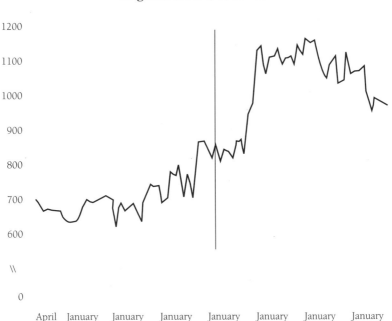

Hagerstown EZ. But the study had been designed to go beyond the statistical analysis to find out whether employers really were responding to the program or to something else. This decision was crucial to reaching a sound conclusion that could inform the debate on EZ legislation.

Results from the surveys of companies in the EZ areas, including both EZ participants and nonparticipants, left some ambiguity about whether any observed growth could be attributed to EZ incentives. Among other things, the survey asked about the relative importance of various factors in influencing these employers' decisions on where to locate. Confirming the usual results of such surveys, such factors as market access and site characteristics outweighed regulatory practices, taxes, financial inducements, and technical assistance—that is, the features associated with EZs—in affecting where businesses locate. On the other hand, a majority of firms participating in the EZs reported that each major incentive included in the Maryland program was at least of moderate importance in their investment and hiring decisions. These rather mixed results clearly left room for doubt about whether the EZ program could be credited with the job growth in Hagerstown.

So, the trend data were examined carefully to identify those firms whose hiring had increased employment in the Hagerstown EZ. Officials of those companies were interviewed to find out whether the EZ incentives were responsible for their actions.

It turned out that the August employment increase was largely due to hiring by one store that had begun full operations at the time. The key question was whether that retailer had done the hiring because of the EZ program. Unfortunately for EZ advocates, the officials reported they had been unaware of the program until after they had made their hiring decisions. Similarly, the October employment rise was mostly accounted for by the decision of one multistate retailer that wanted to fill in a hiatus in its chain of east coast stores and found a suitable vacant building in Hagerstown. In practice, these employers were free riders; that is, they were given tax benefits for doing precisely what they would have done in any case.

Absent these two companies, the postimplementation employment pattern for the Hagerstown EZ looks quite different from that in Figure 5.1. As Figure 5.2 shows, the employment growth from January 1984 until late 1985 appears as the continuation of a trend that began early in 1982. Statistical analysis showed no significant change in the postimplementation period, either in the level or slope of the employment trend. These results suggest that the employment increases in Hagerstown are more likely attributable to recovery from the national recession than to the EZ program. A similar tale could be told about the Salisbury EZ.

Based on this analysis, the GAO concluded that there was no evidence that the Maryland EZ program had stimulated growth in employment in the EZ areas. What is particularly important here is that these results were reached despite the fact that the GAO intentionally selected best-case instances for its

Figure 5.2. Number of Employees for Participants in Hagerstown EZ, with Two Participants Excluded

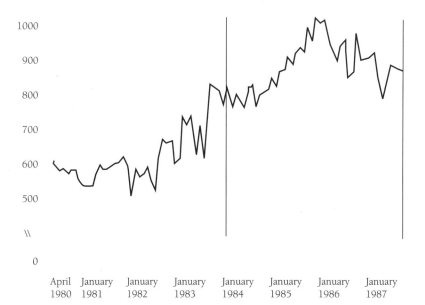

analysis. If EZs of the type proposed in Kemp–Garcia were effective in increasing employment, one would have expected more positive outcomes in these cases.

Furthermore, the results also argued against conducting an analysis of whether EZs reduced transfer payments and increased tax payments by workers (without demonstrated employment growth it would be impossible to identify such outcomes), and also against extending the analysis to nonparticipants located in the EZs, given the findings for participating companies.

The final report recommended a measured approach to developing a federal EZ program. Such a program, it said, should be small-scale, perhaps as part of a demonstration that would allow evaluators to vary systematically independent variables (such as geographic location of EZs and specific benefits) that might affect program outcomes. The GAO also argued for building accountability into the program, including provisions that would prevent businesses from claiming benefits for actions that were incidental to the program, given the appearance of free riders in Maryland.

The Federal EZ Program

With the support of the Clinton Administration, Congress finally provided for a national EZ program in the Omnibus Budget Reconciliation Act of 1993. Under the act, up to 104 zones could be designated, two-thirds of them in urban areas. The Department of Housing and Urban Development would administer the urban zones, and the Department of Agriculture those in rural areas.

This program differs from Kemp–Garcia in two important respects. First, the act creates two tiers of zones, with different packages of benefits: empowerment zones (EZs) and enterprise communities (ECs). And second, it provides for hundreds of millions in direct expenditures over the ten-year authorization of the program. Congress rather ingeniously found this money in the Social Services Block Grant (SSBG) program administered by yet a third department, Health and Human Services. SSBG directs funds to the states to support a variety of social service activities based on a formula (U.S. General Accounting Office, 1997a). This use of direct expenditures is a major break with Kemp's original proposal. Indeed, it is philosophically antithetical to the thrust of Kemp's ideas, which rely on tax incentives to stimulate market-determined investment decisions. Using direct expenditures implies that government—not the market—will make major decisions on what happens in the zones, an approach anathema to supply-side doctrine.

Empowerment zones are eligible for the bulk of both direct expenditures and tax breaks available under the federal program. Urban EZs each are allocated $100 million, and rural EZs $40 million, in SSBG funds over 10 years, while ECs get $3 million each. The federal government also is committed to give the EZs and ECs special consideration in the awarding of competitive funds through other federal programs, help them overcome federal regulatory constraints, and permit them to use federal funds more flexibly (U.S. General Accounting Office, 1997a).

For purposes of this volume, the key support for EZs and ECs comes in the form of tax incentives. Both the EZs and ECs can approve tax-exempt state and local bonds for qualified businesses to finance facilities and land acquisition, up to $20 million in urban and $3 million in rural zones. But businesses in EZs also are eligible for two tax breaks not available in ECs: the Empowerment Zone Employment Credit of up to $3,000 for each employee living and working in the zone, and the Empowerment Zone Expensing Allowance, a special depreciation deduction of up to $20,000 for equipment purchases (U.S. General Accounting Office, 1997a, 1997b).

A total of nine empowerment zones were selected competitively in 1994. Atlanta, Baltimore, Chicago, Detroit, New York, and Philadelphia-Camden were awarded urban EZs; rural EZ designation was awarded to the Kentucky Highlands Investment Corporation, the Mid-Delta (Mississippi) Empowerment Zone Alliance, and the Rio Grande (Texas) Empowerment Zone. In addition, HUD named Los Angeles and Cleveland as "supplemental" EZs, eligible for $125 million and $87 million, respectively, in grants under the department's Economic Development Initiative. It also provided $22 million each from the program for ECs in Boston, Houston, Kansas City, and Oakland. (All but Los Angeles also were eligible for the general EC tax incentives and other benefits.)

This program is far more ambitious than the careful demonstration called for by the GAO. But, significantly, it does include a strong evaluation component. The program requires that the zones identify measurable outcomes and collect data for evaluative purposes. In 1997, HUD contracted with Abt Associates to conduct a five-year evaluation of interim impacts. The GAO also has conducted evaluations of the implementation of the program in both urban (U.S. General Accounting Office, 1997a) and rural (U.S. General Accounting Office, 1997b) areas. The GAO found that urban EZs have not established outcome measures, and that rural EZs and ECs are not providing adequate monitoring information to USDA.

What Are the Lessons for Future Evaluations?

The lessons from this evaluation should be familiar to those who have sampled the evaluation literature over the last decade or so. First, the best outcome evaluation is built on a strong analysis of the underlying processes through which the program works. The GAO was able to disaggregate from the time series the specific employers whose hiring was driving the apparently favorable outcome in two sites, and to use follow-up interviews to test the statistical results. Of course, evaluators of tax expenditures may not always have access to data that allow them to do this. However, whenever possible, they should make every reasonable effort use information on program processes to confirm or disconfirm the results of outcome analyses. In this case, even if the GAO had been unable to find the specific employers responsible for the positive time-series results it could have used its survey findings—suggesting that tax incentives were not especially important influences on business location and hiring decisions—to raise questions about the findings.

Second, the evaluator must be willing to explore and use mixed-methods designs, with multiple data sources and analytic approaches. The evaluation should be driven primarily by the research questions rather than by the familiarity and convenience of data sources. As in the case of this study, developing a useful sampling frame or other data base may require "beating the bushes" for relevant information. It also may require using designs, such as interrupted times series and other quasi-experimental designs, that have not been widely used in tax expenditure evaluations.

Third, obtaining appropriate data for evaluations often requires direct contact with the targets of the intervention in addition to or in lieu of reliance on existing data for secondary analyses. The persons, companies, or other entities who take advantage (or not) of tax expenditure benefits are the ultimate arbiters of whether the intervention achieves its objectives. In the case of the Maryland EZ evaluation, these were the employers located in the EZs. Survey evidence on their perception of the relative importance of EZ provisions on location and hiring decisions was a critical component of the evaluation. (Of course, as a matter of sound policy the perspectives and needs of the targets also should be reflected in the design of tax expenditure programs in the first place.)

Concluding Comments

This evaluation of Maryland enterprise zones provides a rare example of a multimethod prospective evaluation of a tax expenditure program. It highlights the opportunities for adapting the standard evaluation tool kit to analysis of tax expenditures. And it shows how powerful such studies can be. Particularly given the relative paucity of good empirical evaluations at the time it was issued, the GAO report was influential in helping to forestall adoption of a federal enterprise zone program for several years, and the program finally enacted differs greatly from the original proposal. By focusing on one state, burrowing deep into the case study sites, and exploiting the clarity of graphical presentations of the ITS data, the GAO was able to present a credible and understandable story to key policy-makers. And the findings have been cited widely in the subsequent literature on enterprise zones. Policy influence and frequent citation are not bad as hallmarks of success for an evaluation study.

References

Butler, S. M. *Enterprise Zones: A Solution to the Urban Crisis?* Washington, D.C.: The Heritage Foundation, 1979.

Butler, S. M. "The Conceptual Evolution of Enterprise Zones." In R. E. Green (ed.), *Enterprise Zones: New Directions in Economic Development.* Newbury Park, Calif.: Sage Publications, 1991, pp. 27–40.

Cook, T. D., and Campbell, D. T. *Quasi-experimentation: Design and Analysis Issues for Field Settings.* Chicago: Rand McNally, 1979.

Grasso, P. G. "Distributive Policies and the Politics of Economic Development." In S. Redburn, T. F. Buss, and L. Ledebur (eds.), *Revitalizing the American Economy.* New York: Associated Faculty Press, 1986.

Hall, P. "Green Fields and Grey Areas." *Papers of the RTPI Annual Conference, Chester.* London: Royal Town Planning Institute, 1977. Reprinted in *The Enterprise Zones Concept: British Origins and American Adaptations.* Berkeley: University of California Press, 1981.

Hanson, S. B. "Comparing Enterprise Zones to Other Economic Development Techniques." In R. E. Green (ed.), *Enterprise Zones: New Directions in Economic Development.* Newbury Park, Calif.: Sage Publications, 1991, pp. 7–26.

Levitan, S. A. "Evaluation of Federal Social Programs: An Uncertain Impact." Occasional Paper 1992–2 (June). Washington, D.C.: Center for Social Policy Studies, George Washington University, 1992.

Levitan, S. A., and Miller, E. I. "Enterprise Zones Are No Solution for Our Blighted Areas." *Challenge,* May/June 1992, pp. 4–8.

McCleary, R., and Hay, R. *Applied Time Series Analysis for the Social Sciences.* Beverly Hills, Calif.: Sage Publications, 1980.

Spilberg, P., and Kern, C. "Enterprise Zone Tax Incentives: Their Value to Firms and Their Cost to the Federal Government." Unpublished manuscript. Washington, 1982.

U.S. General Accounting Office. *Enterprise Zones: Lessons From the Maryland Experience.* Washington, D.C.: U.S. General Accounting Office, 1988. (GAO/PEMD-89–2)

U.S. General Accounting Office. *Case Study Evaluations.* Washington, D.C.: U.S. General Accounting Office, 1990a. (Transfer Paper 10.1.9)

U.S. General Accounting Office. *Prospective Evaluation Methods: The Prospective Evaluation Synthesis.* Washington, D.C.: U.S. General Accounting Office, 1990b. (Transfer Paper 10.1.10)

U.S. General Accounting Office. *Community Development: Status of Urban Empowerment Zones.* Washington, D.C.: U.S. General Accounting Office, 1997a. (GAO/RCED-92–21)

U.S. General Accounting Office. *Rural Development: New Approach to Empowering Communities Needs Refinement.* Washington, D.C.: U.S. General Accounting Office, 1997b. (GAO/RCED-97–75)

Yin, R. K. *Case Study Research: Design and Methods,* rev. ed. Beverly Hills, Calif.: Sage, 1989.

SCOTT CROSSE *is a senior research analyst in the Human Services Group at Westat. In recent years, he has conducted evaluations of substance abuse prevention and treatment programs.*

PATRICK G. GRASSO *is senior knowledge management officer in the operations evaluation department of The World Bank, after serving as an assistant director of the Program Evaluation and Methodology Division of the U.S. General Accounting Office.*

MONICA KELLY *is a senior evaluator in the National Security and International Affairs Division of the U.S. General Accounting Office. Recently she has evaluated the potential benefits and risks of incorporating commercial procurement practices into the Department of Defense weapons procurement process.*

The investment tax credit is a familiar example of a tax expenditure.
The evaluation of its effectiveness described in this chapter provides a
model for evaluating other tax expenditures.

The Investment Tax Credit

Thomas Karier

According to the Revenue Act of 1962, the purpose of the investment tax credit (ITC) was "to encourage modernization and expansion of the Nation's productive facilities and thereby improve the economic potential of the country, with a resultant increase in job opportunities and betterment of our competitive position in the world economy."

As evident from this quote, high expectations accompanied the passage of the investment tax credit in 1962. But did the ITC accomplish these goals or did it merely enrich those corporations with a natural proclivity toward high equipment investments? In order for the credit to succeed businesses had to respond to the ITC by increasing their outlays on productive equipment. President Kennedy's economic advisors were confident that this would happen. But what if equipment prices were not particularly important in investment decisions? Or what if the significance of the ITC was limited to the accounting department and did not affect management decisions? Instead of leading to a "modernization and expansion of the Nation's productive facilities," the ITC would merely reduce taxes for some corporations.

A tax expenditure, like the investment tax credit, reduces the tax liability of a particular taxpayer, in this case equipment buyers. During some years, the ITC reduced taxes by a significant amount. For example, in 1981 corporations claimed $19 billion for investment tax credits, more than the entire amount spent on the U.S. Department of Energy that year. In a sense, the government paid $19 billion for equipment owned by private businesses. Was this a good use of tax dollars? Did the investment tax credit result in more investment

---

This article was adapted from "Investment Tax Credit Reconsidered," Thomas Karier, The Jerome Levy Economics Institute of Bard College, Policy Brief No. 13.

spending than what would otherwise have occurred? In all likelihood there will probably always be some doubt about the answer to this question. We can not rerun history without the credit and measure the change in equipment expenditures. The best we can do is to logically evaluate the policy in terms of what it was intended to accomplish and how that was expected to occur.

About the Credit

There are few macroeconomic disorders for which a large injection of investment spending is not considered a suitable remedy. It would be difficult to exaggerate the range of benefits commonly attributed to investment spending. Given the goal of expanding investment spending, how does one ensure that it will be forthcoming in sufficient quantity? Only government investment, including education, infrastructure, and research, is amenable to direct and immediate manipulation. Most of the remaining investment in the private sector is determined by the disparate actions of hundreds of large firms, and to a lesser degree, hundreds of smaller ones. Efforts to promote investment in the private sector have, by necessity, resorted to indirect measures such as tax incentives.

An important experiment in economic policy took place between 1962 and 1986 with the implementation of the investment tax credit. During this period, firms were permitted a credit against their income tax liability equivalent to a percentage of their investment in machinery, equipment, or furniture. Excluded from the tax credit were buildings, structural components, and intangible property. Through this tax expenditure, the federal government provided corporations with billions of dollars in credit in hope of raising the level of investment in equipment.

How Is It Intended to Work?

There are three primary ways in which the investment tax credit is believed to stimulate investment. Two are microeconomic responses and one is macroeconomic. In the macroeconomic mechanism, any tax cut will have a positive impact on the economy by means of stimulating aggregate demand. Despite compelling historical support for this viewpoint, not all economists are equally receptive to the idea. Because this is not a debate on macroeconomic theory, this study will focus instead on the two microeconomic mechanisms. However, it is probably safe to presume that the multiplier effect of the ITC resembles that of any other corporate tax cut. To the extent that any corporate tax cut will stimulate purchases and production, so will the ITC.

The two microeconomic effects are defined as the price effect and the income effect. The price effect is the simple idea that consumers and businesses will buy more of anything when it is cheaper. Because the ITC lowers the price of equipment, businesses are expected to buy more of it based on the price effect. In practice, the actual response may still be insignificant if either the change in the price is small or the demand is relatively unresponsive to price changes. Empirical evidence is required to determine the response.

A second possible means by which an investment credit can affect investment is through the *income effect* or, as it is sometimes called, the cash flow effect. By this mechanism, a firm qualifying for the tax credit reduces its tax liability, thus raising its income. This income is then available for capital investment. But it can also be used for other purposes, including paying higher wages or dividends, making financial investments, buying back outstanding stock or bonds, or financing acquisitions. The question concerning the income effect is: how much of the additional corporate income is spent on capital investment and how much on these other areas?

A summary of the price and income effects is pictured in Figure 6.1. The price effect runs directly from the ITC to a reduction in the effective price of

Figure 6.1. Investment Tax Credit: Relationship to Equipment Investment

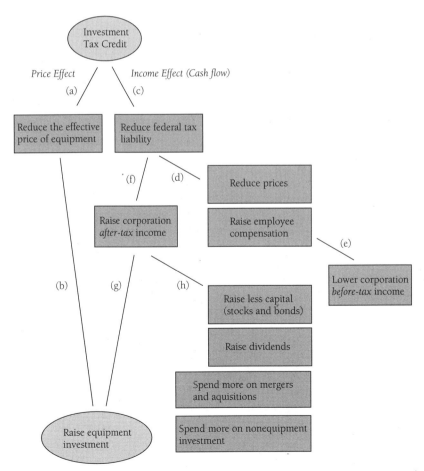

equipment to raising equipment investment (a and b). The income effect (c) is more complicated because there are many alternative ways for companies to spend the tax saving from the ITC. The first option is for the company to lower prices for consumers or raise employee compensation (d). This is one way to "use up" the tax savings, one that would also reduce corporate before-tax income (e). This possibility is tested later. If companies don't lower prices or raise compensation, then after-tax income is likely to rise (f). This income may be spent on equipment (g) or on any number of other areas including dividends, mergers and acquisitions, nonequipment investment, or reducing the need to sell stocks and bonds (h). These possibilities are also tested later.

What Are the Central Issues in Evaluating the Investment Tax Credit?

The most difficult policy to assess is one that never changes over time. Fortunately this is not the case for the investment tax credit. After being introduced in 1962, the credit was suspended from October 1966 to March 1967, terminated from April 1969 to August 1971, and finally eliminated in 1986. What began as a 7 percent credit in 1962 was increased to 10 percent in 1975. In addition, the original law in 1962 required a reduction in the depreciable or basis value of the investment equivalent to the size of the credit. This requirement was dropped in 1964 and partially reinstated in 1982 with a required reduction in basis value equivalent to half the credit. Additional restrictions were applied to certain industries as well as to short-lived assets and investments outside the United States. All of these changes and qualifications may have created headaches for tax accountants but they enriched the quality of the experiment by increasing the variation in the credits over time.

Determining causality is always the most difficult part of assessing any public policy, especially tax expenditures. The approach taken in this research is to look for the most obvious evidence first and then focus in on the detail as necessary. If the investment tax credit had a significant effect on equipment investment, then the most obvious result to look for is an increase in equipment investment during the years that the ITC was in place. The second step involves details about how the tax credit was expected to work as outlined in Figure 6.1. These specific mechanisms are evaluated later in this research, providing more depth about the effectiveness of the credit.

The Evidence

One of the first questions that arises is how to measure equipment investment and the ITC. It is generally expected that equipment investment, like many other economic activities, will rise in proportion to the overall growth in the economy. An increase in equipment investment over the past thirty years would not be surprising given the great increase in the gross domestic product (GDP). The fact that the ITC provided a unique benefit for equipment investment suggests that equipment expenditures should have risen relative to the GDP. This suggests that equipment investment should be measured relative to the GDP. In this study equipment investment is divided by the GDP after correcting both measures separately for inflation. This latter step is important because equipment and the GDP experienced different inflation rates.

Measuring the ITC presents a different kind of problem. Although the ITC existed in some years and not in others, it also changed in the years that it did apply. The most direct way to capture the intensity of the ITC is to divide the total amount of credits claimed in any given year by the total value of equipment investment in that year. This represents an annual average value for the ITC. These are the values graphed in Figure 6.2.

Equipment shares. The historical pattern between equipment investment and the investment tax credit (ITC) is presented in Figure 6.2. The pattern for the ITC in the figure captures several important events: the suspension from 1969 to 1971, the increase from 7 percent to 10 percent in 1975, and the final repeal in 1986. The figure also shows that real equipment spending climbed erratically from 4.4 percent in 1961 to 7.6 percent in 1992. If the data had ended in 1985, they would have provided a compelling case for the investment tax credit. It would have appeared that the credit interrupted a downward trend in investment spending from 1946 to 1961 and in fact coincided with a steady increase from 1962 to 1985. However, the graph does not end in 1985 and what happened after that is critical. Despite the repeal of the ITC in 1986, the share of equipment investment remained relatively high from 1987 to 1992. Even in the absence of the ITC, companies continued to spend as much on equipment as they had under the incentive of the ITC. This raises a strong possibility that other, more important factors were behind the rise in equipment spending from 1962 to 1985.

One variable that must be considered is the average price of equipment. As can be seen in Figure 6.3, the upward trend in equipment prices from 1947 to 1961 coincides with a period of falling equipment investment relative to the GDP. Businesses appeared to invest relatively less in equipment during this time because it was more expensive. Even more important is that the ensuing period of falling equipment prices from 1962 to 1992 coincided with an expansion in real equipment investment. Price appears to have an important effect on equipment investments. This raises an important question: did businesses raise equipment spending between 1962 and 1992 because of the lower average prices or because of the ITC? The answer is not obvious from these graphs and requires a more comprehensive approach.

Statistical Analysis

When more than one variable can account for an historical event, a logical test involves multiple regression. This is the approach taken here. Both equipment

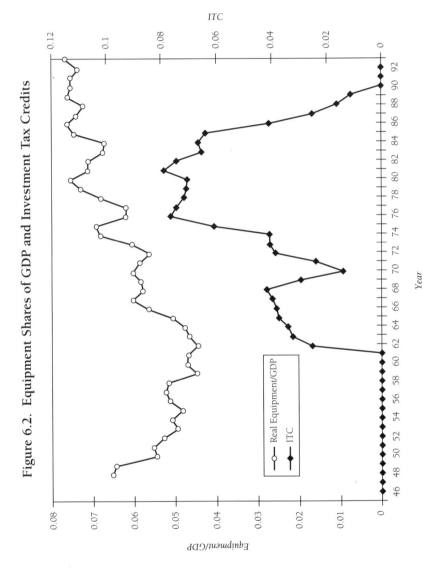

Figure 6.2. Equipment Shares of GDP and Investment Tax Credits

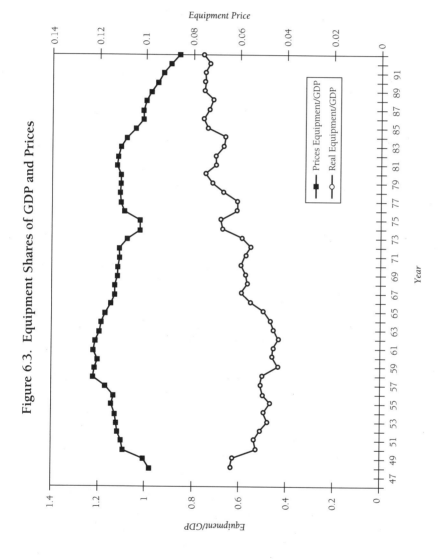

Figure 6.3. Equipment Shares of GDP and Prices

prices and the investment tax credit are included because they fall into the category of cost of capital variables. Other cost-of-capital variables include real interest rates and marginal tax rates. Capital is relatively cheaper when marginal tax rates, interest rates, and equipment prices are lower. Other variables that could influence equipment investment are corporate cash flow, which captures the income effect, and capacity utilization. It is anticipated that firms will be more likely to invest after excess capacity has been exhausted.

For the most part, the variables and analysis follow conventional methods. There is, however, one innovation that warrants an explanation. Indices of capital costs typically combine several parameters, such as capital prices, tax rates, real interest rates, and tax credits into a single annual value. In fact, this method produces a single value that is equivalent to an annual rent payment whose present value over the lifetime of the equipment—properly discounted for time, depreciation, and future taxes—is equal to the current price (Hall and Jorgenson, 1967). It is easy to forget that at any moment in time, a firm only knows the purchase price and tax credit for certain; all other variables, such as real interest and tax rates, apply to the future and are unknown. Consequently, the approach taken in this chapter is to include each variable separately, under the presumption that assigning arbitrary values to unknown variables contaminates the indices. The advantage of this approach is that it imposes the fewest assumptions in regard to how firms actually process current information in developing future expectations.

One of the cost-of-capital variables is the real interest rate, which is represented by the prime rate of interest less the rate of inflation (GDP deflator). Another cost-of-capital variable is the corporate tax rate, which is equal to the statutory tax rate on corporate income. Equipment prices are represented by the ratio of the price deflator for producer's durable equipment to the deflator for GDP. In addition, the investment tax credit is included as the ratio of total corporate investment tax credits divided by producer's durable equipment.

Other variables include capacity utilization for manufacturing and cash flow, equivalent to the sum of consumption of fixed capital for corporations and undistributed corporate profits. The dependent variable, equipment investment, was adjusted for inflation and then divided by the GDP, similarly adjusted. All of the variables were obtained from the National Income Product Accounts published by the Department of Commerce, except for the prime interest rate and capacity utilization, which were obtained from the Economic Report to the President, 1993, published by the U.S. Government Printing Office.

The results of this statistical analysis demonstrate that investment levels are significantly higher when capacity utilization is high or equipment prices are low. Tax credits, whether included separately or in the full model, do not appear to have a significant effect on levels of equipment investment. The coefficient on investment tax credits was not significantly different from zero in either case. The coefficients on marginal tax rates, cash flow, and real interest rates were neither significant nor always the expected sign. There is no compelling evidence here of a strong impact of investment tax credits on levels of investment spending.

The absence of a strong positive effect of tax credits on equipment investment is an important result. However, it raises an equally important question. Why does equipment investment appear to be influenced by prices but not by the ITC? After all, the ITC alters the effective price of equipment and one would expect price and the ITC to have similar effects. One possibility is that the ITC was relatively smaller than the price changes. Prices fell by approximately 30 percent compared to the ITC of 10 percent. There is also the possibility that managers did not understand what their accounting departments clearly did: the ITC made equipment purchases 10 percent cheaper. A final possibility is that businesses bought more equipment between 1962 and 1992 because the equipment was better rather than cheaper. In fact the price decrease may have simply reflected an adjustment for improved quality. Whatever the reason, the results of this work indicate that market price or quality had a significant impact on equipment investment but government policy did not.

Composition of Investment

The ITC can also alter the composition of investment. If the ITC encouraged a disproportional investment in equipment, then we would expect to see equipment increase relative to other business investments such as nonresidential fixed investment. Figure 6.4 summarizes these data. It shows producers' durable equipment as a share of nonresidential investment, both corrected separately for inflation. The ratio rose from 49 percent in 1961 to 73 percent in 1992. The investment tax credit from Figure 6.2 is also reproduced here. It should be evident from the figure that the composition of investment shifted toward equipment when the investment tax credit was in effect. Once again, if the data stopped in 1985, the effectiveness of the ITC would be confirmed. But contrary to this hypothesis, investment became even more equipment-intensive after the credit was repealed in 1986.

Prices again show up as a strong competing variable. As shown in Figure 6.4, equipment prices relative to nonresidential investment fell gradually from the early 1960s to the present. Separate statistical analysis shows that relative prices are statistically significant in a model that explains 93 percent of the variation in equipment composition. The investment tax credit, however, had the wrong sign and was insignificant. It does not appear that the presence of the investment tax credit caused any significant increase in equipment investment.

We are left to conclude that equipment expenditures increased relative to other investments and relative to GDP due to falling equipment prices rather than the ITC. In contrast, an earlier study by Hall and Jorgenson (1967) concluded that, "the investment tax credit has been a potent stimulus to the level of investment; it also shifted the composition of investment toward equipment." The difference is that they combined the two variables, the ITC and

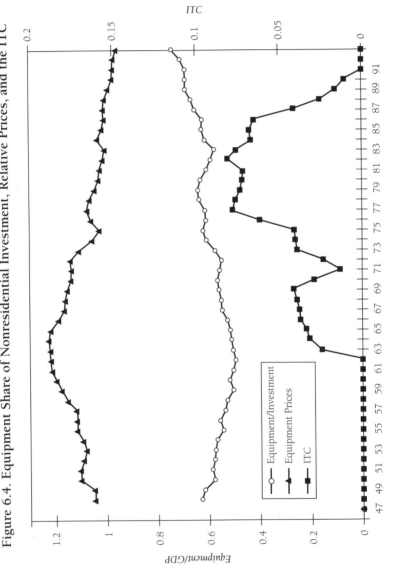

Figure 6.4. Equipment Share of Nonresidential Investment, Relative Prices, and the ITC

equipment prices in their analysis. Only by separating them is it clear that the effects were in fact different.

Income Effect

The same regression analysis used to check the effect of prices and the ITC did not support the finding of a positive income effect. The coefficient on the cash flow variable was not statistically significant. It is possible to investigate this finding in more detail. In theory, it is conceivable that a larger corporate tax refund would be spent on more investment but there are other possibilities, as summarized in Figure 6.1. The goal of the tax credit could be entirely frustrated if the tax savings was used to pay higher dividends, buy back outstanding stock or debt, acquire competing firms, or replace more conventional sources of investment funds. Is there any evidence that this is in fact the case?

Tracing the income effect of a tax expenditure. When a corporation receives a tax reduction, how does it respond? Consider the possibility that tax credits are distributed to either consumers or employees in the form of lower prices or higher salaries. What are the chances that a company would respond to a lucrative tax break in this manner? Most people would consider the price cut to be unlikely. But remember that many analysts readily accept the view that tax increases are passed on to consumers in *higher* prices. If this is true then it is possible that tax cuts or credits could be passed back to consumers in *lower* prices. If the burden of the corporate profit tax is shifted to consumers or employees then it is at least conceivable that tax credits provide relief to the same parties. The relevance to this thesis is that whatever portion of a tax credit is shifted in this manner will not be available for additional investment.

How do you determine whether tax cuts or credits are passed back to consumers or employees? If they were passed back, then corporate tax cuts, of which there have been many, would coincide with *decreases* in before-tax profits. Essentially businesses would be exchanging their lower tax burden for lower prices or higher salaries, thus reducing their before-tax profits. Is this actually what happened when corporate taxes were cut between 1945 and 1995?

The relationship between corporate profits before taxes relative to GDP and average tax rates is presented in Figure 6.5. As illustrated by the figure, profit shares mirror the business cycle and experienced a one-time drop around 1970. After averaging approximately 11 percent from 1946 to 1970, the profit share slid to about 9 percent from 1970 to 1992. Average tax rates also declined during the period. They fell from over 50 percent in 1951 to less than 30 percent in 1992. The question is: did corporations distribute the tax savings to consumers and employees, thus reducing their profits before-taxes?

There are two reasons to believe this was not the case. First, the pattern of decline in profit shares does not match the pattern of decline in tax rates. Whereas profit shares appear to shift to a new, lower average around 1970, the decline in tax rates is concentrated in three distinct periods: 1951 to 1954, 1960 to 1965, and 1980 to 1983.

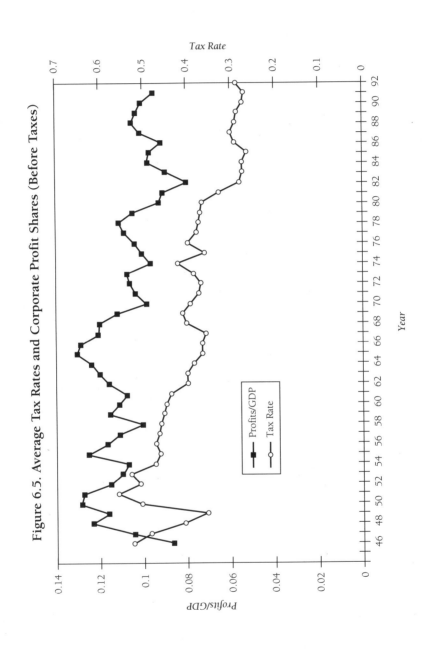

Figure 6.5. Average Tax Rates and Corporate Profit Shares (Before Taxes)

A second objection is that most of the variation in profit shares can easily be accounted for by other factors. Changes in capacity utilization directly affect profit shares and explain much of their movement over the business cycle. Profit shares are also affected by the level of price competition in the United States, which accelerated with the growth of imports.

A statistical test shows that these two variables, capacity utilization and import shares of the gross domestic product, can account for approximately 81 percent of the variation in profit shares over this period. The predicted values of this simple model are compared to the actual values in Figure 6.6. This illustrates that there is very little variation for tax rates to explain once these other variables are accounted for. (Karier, 1994).

All of this evidence points to the conclusion that reductions in the corporate tax rate, including investment tax credits, are not for the most part passed on to consumers and employees. Instead, firms are left with relatively higher after-tax income, which is at least available to finance additional investment. This brings us to the next question: were the savings from the investment tax credit spent on equipment investment or, for that matter, any other kind of productive investment?

Dividends

As a practical matter, some fraction of after-tax income is likely to be distributed directly to shareholders in the form of dividends. The actual fraction of profits distributed to shareholders has fluctuated between 40 and 80 percent between 1946 and 1992, as reported in Figure 6.7. At this rate, dividends can absorb a large part of the tax savings intended to raise investment. The fraction of profits after taxes actually distributed as dividends. In the 1980s and 1990s approximately 60 percent of after-tax income was paid out in dividends, compared to approximately 45 percent during the 1950s, 1960s, and 1970s. In addition to this general increase, dividend shares tend to move counter-cyclically, rising in recessions and falling in expansions. A simple statistical analysis covering 1946 to 1992 shows that for every dollar increase in after-tax profits, dividends increased by 56 cents.

This does not necessarily mean that 56 percent of the savings from an investment tax credit will be distributed as dividends. The actual amount could be more or less, but this provides a useful benchmark.

Other Uses for Tax Savings

There is no assurance that even if tax savings are withheld from shareholders, that they will be devoted exclusively to additional real investment. The funds made available from tax credits could be used by a company to purchase its own stocks or bonds or to finance a merger or take-over. It is equally possible that these funds would simply supplant other sources of investment funds such as the sale of debt or equity. Each of these diversions summarized in Figure 6.1

Figure 6.6. Corporate Profit Shares (Before Taxes), Actual and Predicted

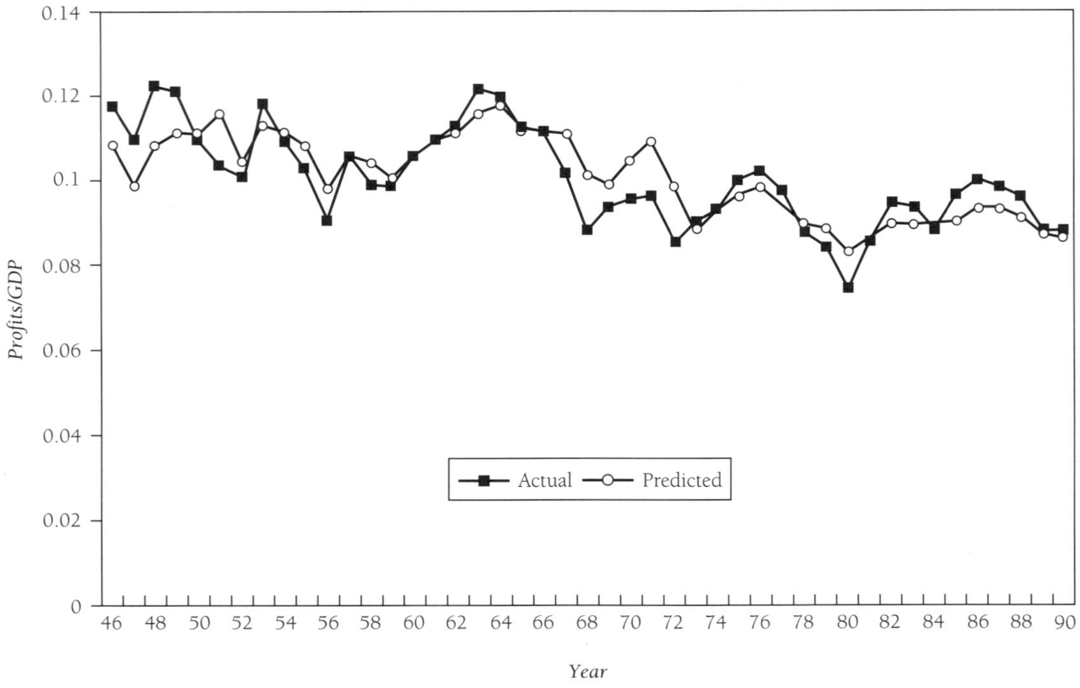

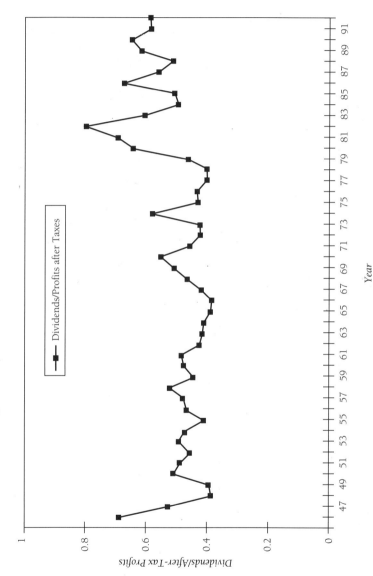

Figure 6.7. Dividends as a Share of After-Tax Profits

(h) tends to dilute the amount of the tax credit ultimately spent on new investment.

How much of after-tax profits are diverted and how much spent on real property, plant, and equipment? A direct way to investigate this question is to look at the behavior of a large number of firms. For this purpose, a sample was drawn of 1,837 companies from Compustat Database for 1991. Compustat is a comprehensive source of financial data covering a large number of corporations. It is produced by Standard & Poor's which is a division of The McGraw-Hill Company.

Several tests were conducted. The first investigated how much more likely firms were to make investments if they had a high cash flow from depreciation, ordinary income, and extraordinary income, and a high inflow of funds from the sale of stocks and bonds. Because the tax credit is most likely to raise ordinary income, this is the key variable for this study. All of these variables were divided by company net sales to obtain shares. Ordinary income was measured after taxes but before extraordinary items and investment was equal to capital expenditure on property, plant, and equipment.

The results of this test show that a firm with a dollar more of income after taxes spends only twelve cents more on property, plant, and equipment. The obvious question is why investment spending goes up so little. From additional tests we know that approximately 40 cents of a dollar more in income are spent on dividends. We also find that firms with higher income tend to reduce their sale of securities which fund investments. The finding is that a firm with a dollar more income will reduce its sales of stock by 21 cents and debt by 17 cents. The conclusion is that firms with relatively higher after-tax income distribute more dividends and sell relatively fewer securities. The amount that trickles down into additional investment is not large.

This detailed investigation of the income effect reaffirms the statistical results reported in the previous section, which found that cash flow was not a particularly important determinant of equipment investment. It seems reasonable to expect that the tax credit raises after-tax profits, much of which is then distributed to stockholders. The remaining amount may be spent on investments but the overall impact diminishes as firms simply sell fewer securities to fund investment. If the purpose of tax credit was to provide corporations with more money to invest then it was not very efficient.

Why Investment?

There are two very different views about why equipment investment is important. One view is that equipment investment, more than any other type of investment, creates the potential for great economic growth. This was the conclusion reached in an article by De Long and Summers (1991). The authors claimed that countries with a relatively high level of equipment investment also experienced relatively high growth rates. The surprising result was that this relationship held only for equipment investment and not for related investments in structures. If this were true, then shifting the nation's resources in favor of equipment, at the expense of everything else, would pay off in higher growth.

As compelling as De Long and Summers' international study was, the evidence does not transfer easily to the United States. The beneficial effect of high levels of equipment investment spending is unfortunately not as readily apparent for the United States from 1950 to 1992. Figure 6.8 shows the ratio of spending for durable equipment to the GDP and the growth rates of real GDP, calculated as five-year moving averages. Although equipment spending went up, average growth rates went down. There is little evidence in this figure that high levels of private investment in equipment are associated with strong economic growth.

There are of course other factors that would tend to raise or lower GDP growth rates, but this preliminary evidence raises some serious questions. At the very least it points out the need to explain why strong equipment growth in the United States from 1962 to 1992 did not translate into high economic growth.

Another view of why equipment spending is important is because it can affect aggregate demand in the short run and boost a lagging economy. In this Keynesian view, a change in equipment investment should be directly correlated with immediate changes in the GDP. This familiar fact is illustrated by the close relationship between the percentage changes in annual real growth rates of GDP and the percentage changes in real equipment investment between 1948 and 1993. Annual changes in real equipment investment are closely related to annual changes in real GDP. It may be difficult to sort out the causality in this relationship but at least some part of it can be attributed to the fact that rapid changes in investment spending can alter the trajectory of economic growth. In this lies a paramount need for public policy: to compensate for the volatility of private sector investment.

Tax Credits as a Countercyclical Tool

Does the historical record have anything to say about the effectiveness of an investment tax credit as a countercyclical tool? Is it possible to use tax credits to encourage equipment spending only in those years that it is needed? In fact, the investment tax credit was actually used to counter the business cycle during its first few years of its existence. It was initially deployed when investment was relatively low and then revoked twice: in 1966 and 1969, when investment showed signs of recovering. But between reinstatement in 1971 and repeal in 1986, the credit was offered in good times and bad. The end of the credit as a countercyclical policy after 1971 marked a victory for the business sector, which had from the start insisted on a permanent tax cut.

There appears to be a legitimate and useful role for public policy in stimulating investment, especially during periods of economic recession. The problem with the tax credit is that the historical evidence does not demonstrate a clear impact on private investment. Furthermore it would not make a very use-

Figure 6.8. Real GDP Growth and Equipment Shares of GDP

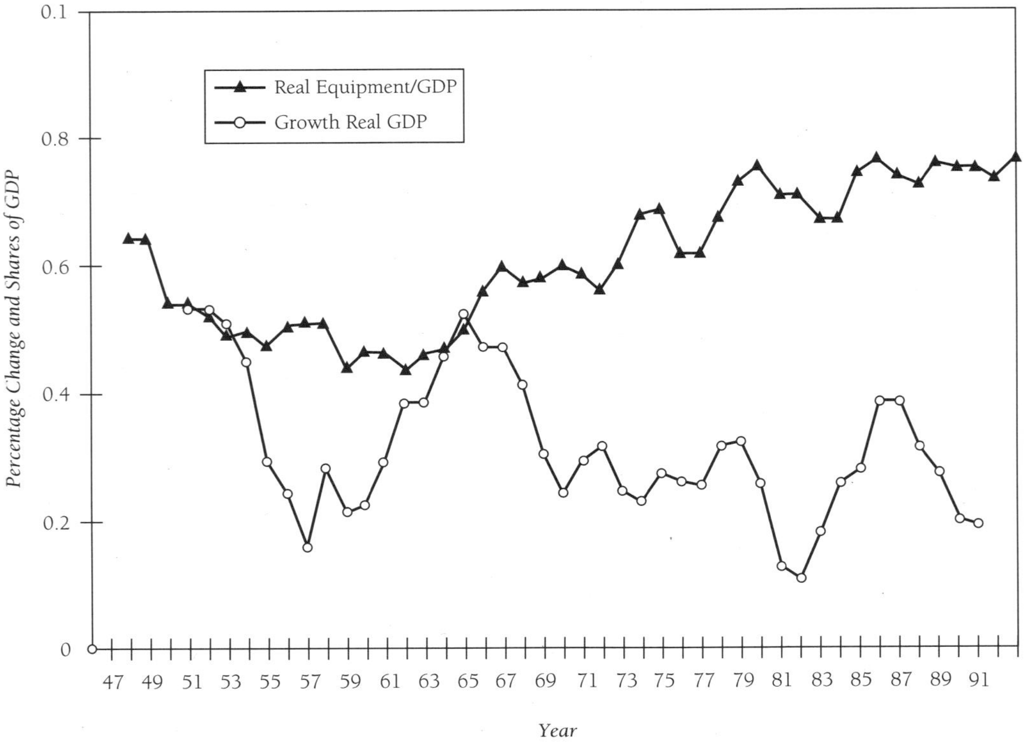

ful countercyclical tool. Businesses object to rapid variations in the tax structure, which add another level of uncertainty to their investment decisions. There is something to be said for not adding any more uncertainty to a decision that already faces significant uncertainties from the private market.

Policy Implications

For more than twenty years, the federal government provided corporations with billions of dollars of tax credits in the hope of raising the level of investment in equipment. According to the evidence presented here, these credits did not have a perceptible impact on either the composition of investment or the proportion of national output dedicated to equipment investment.

These observations were reinforced by more detailed investigations into how tax credits are supposed to work. Although the tax credit was supposed to increase the importance of equipment in total nonresidential investment, the evidence is lacking. Furthermore, although some of the credit may be spent directly on additional investment, that amount may be minuscule. The estimate in this study found that 12 cents of every additional dollar of after-tax income was spent on property plant and equipment. The remainder is typically used to pay higher dividends, buy stocks or bonds, or release firms from the need to sell as much debt or equity.

Much of the evidence presented here in regard to the investment tax credit has a direct relevance to the effectiveness of other corporate tax breaks. Marginal tax rates on corporate income have declined steadily over the past forty years, and yet the evidence in this research does not show any perceptible response in higher equipment investment. Generous depreciation rates have increased corporate cash flow, but only a small fraction of this is likely to see its way into new investment.

Although investment tax credits may not contribute much to economic growth, there is no reason to abandon the effort to stimulate investment, both for countering the business cycle and for creating new job opportunities. The failure of tax incentives to stimulate private sector investment only means that future efforts may be more successful if they concentrate on raising public sector investment. It is important, if not obvious, that a dollar spent on public investment will produce a dollar of public investment. There are more than a few promising opportunities for public investment in education, infrastructure, and research and development.

Public investment can be financed by rearranging current budget priorities and augmented during recessions with deficit spending. But it is difficult to imagine that public investment could attain adequate levels without a tax increase. In this regard, particular attention should be directed to the corporate income tax. This tax has fallen to historic lows and if revived could provide important revenue to finance a broad program of public investment. Although critics will decry the adverse impact of corporate tax increases on investment, the historical record examined in this chapter suggests otherwise.

If such an important tax break as the investment tax credit failed to stimulate investment, why would the elimination of other tax breaks depress them? After all, if corporate tax breaks had met their objective— higher economic growth—public investment would be less urgent today.

Evaluation Methodology

The method employed to evaluate the ITC for this research was intended to be logical and reasonably plausible. An alternative approach, employed by some earlier studies, is to construct a comprehensive theoretical model and then use the model to test policies. A good example of this latter approach was used by Hall and Jorgenson to evaluate the ITC in 1967. They constructed a very concise microeconomic model premised on perfect information and profit maximization. As they constructed the model they added additional assumptions as required. The layers of assumptions become cumulative and the credibility of the results depended entirely on the plausibility of these many assumptions. Unfortunately, the statistical application tested the policies, not the model. Without any basis for accepting the model, one is left with no basis for accepting the results.

The approach in this chapter is more empirical and relies less on models and assumptions. It begins with an obvious question: did equipment investment increase during the years that the ITC was in place? A second obvious question concerns other factors that may affect investment and may be even more important. These would include the level of economic activity (GDP) and equipment prices. We did not calculate a single cost of capital index like Hall and Jorgenson did, because this can only be done by introducing controversial assumptions. Instead, many of the same components of the cost of capital were included in this study, but they were included separately.

A second feature of this study is that it began with a comprehensive mapping of all plausible mechanisms by which the ITC could possibly increase equipment spending. This helped to focus the research and make sure that no reasonable possibility was overlooked.

Once the mechanisms were outlined, it was important to consider what data would be most appropriate to investigate the relationship. For the first, general question concerning the historical effectiveness of the ITC, the appropriate data appeared to be national time series. This was especially appropriate in this case because both the ITC and equipment spending did change over the period of time that data were available. Also the data were publicly available from the Department of Commerce and the Internal Revenue Service, and are widely credible among academic and government researchers.

Questions about the income effect and the role of cash-flow variables seemed to gravitate toward the behavior of individual firms. Compustat is a particularly comprehensive source of information on individual corporations and has also earned considerable respect among researchers. Much of the financial data included in this source are mandated for government reporting purposes or are routinely included in annual corporate reports.

Whenever the issue of causality is involved there will always be room for honest disagreement. No statistical test can definitively establish causality, but statistical evidence is always worth considering and, at its best, is not easily ignored.

References

Compustat. New York: Standard and Poor's Compustat Services (various years).

Council of Economic Advisers. Economic Report of the President. Washington, D.C.: U.S. Government Printing Office, 1993.

De Long, J. B., and Summers, L. "Equipment Investment and Economic Growth." *The Quarterly Journal of Economics,* May 1991, pp. 445–502.

Hall, R., and Jorgenson, D. "Tax Policy and Investment Behavior." *American Economic Review,* 1967, 57, 391–414.

Karier, T. "Investment Tax Credit Reconsidered: Business Tax Incentives and Investments." Annandale, NY: Jerome Levy Economics Institute of Bard College, 1994. (Public Policy Brief, No. 13)

U.S. Department of Commerce. *National Income and Product Accounts of the United States.* Washington, D.C.: U.S. Government Printing Office (various years).

THOMAS KARIER is associate dean and economics professor at Eastern Washington University and a research associate at the Jerome Levy Economics Institute of Bard College, Annandale, New York.

Flow-through shares are an income tax incentive for certain equity investments in mining and energy companies in Canada. This chapter describes this tax incentive and discusses an evaluation of its performance conducted by the Department of Finance Canada.

A Canadian Tax Incentive for Equity Investments in Mining and Energy Companies

Gordon J. Lenjosek

Flow-through shares are one of several ways in which mining and energy companies can finance exploration and development activities and certain renewable energy, energy conservation, and energy efficiency activities in Canada. These equity instruments receive special income tax treatment and are issued by means of agreements between eligible companies and their investors. An investor who purchases a flow-through share in a mining or energy company under such an agreement receives both an equity interest in the company and the right to claim income tax deductions associated with new expenditures incurred by the company on eligible capital costs. Proceeds from any subsequent sale of the equity interest are treated as a capital gain, a portion of which (currently 75 percent) is included in the investor's taxable income. In exchange for transferring (or renouncing) the eligible expenses (and the right to the associated income tax deductions) to investors, a mining or energy company receives for its flow-through shares the price of its common shares plus a premium based on the tax value to the investor of the transferred expenses.

Recent Canadian federal budgets have refocused and extended the types of expenditures that companies can renounce to investors under flow-through

This chapter is based on an evaluation of flow-through shares published by the Department of Finance Canada in October 1994. The author wishes to thank Don MacDonald, Bill Toms, and Geoff Trueman for their helpful suggestions. The views expressed in this chapter are the responsibility of the author alone.

share agreements. Prior to the 1996 budget, eligible expenditures were limited to those incurred by mining and petroleum companies and included Canadian exploration expense (fully deductible in a year), Canadian development expense (deductible at an annual rate of 30 percent on a declining balance basis), and Canadian oil and gas property expense (deductible at an annual rate of 10 percent on a declining balance basis). The 1996 budget made Canadian development expense relating to mineral property costs and Canadian oil and gas property expense ineligible for flow-through share treatment. That budget and others announced the extension of the flow-through share provisions to a new income tax category of expenses termed Canadian renewable and conservation expense (fully deductible in a year).

The flow-through share financing mechanism can be thought of as consisting of three fundamental components: (1) a financing structure, specifically the flow-through share agreement between the mining or energy company and the investor; (2) an expenses-for-shares transaction, which itself consists of three components: the exchange of consideration for new shares, the incurring of eligible expenses by the mining or energy company, and the renunciation of the eligible expenses to the investor; and (3) income tax recognition of the renunciation of eligible expenses where certain conditions are met concerning the expenses-for-shares transaction and the reporting of information in respect of both the flow-through share agreement and the renunciation.

Investors can purchase flow-through shares either directly from mining or energy companies or indirectly through, for example, limited partnerships, which in turn acquire flow-through shares from such companies. The latter mechanism was the more popular of the two during the flow-through share boom in the middle and late 1980s. (Jog, Lenjosek, and McKenzie, 1996, footnote 2, p. 1018, describe the way in which limited partnership intermediaries generally operate.) The key advantages of a limited partnership are that it provides investors with portfolio diversification and risk reduction, but leaves the choice of individual investments in the hands of professional managers.

For investors, flow-through shares are an alternative type of equity investment that offers substantial liquidity, is tax-advantaged relative to other forms of risk capital, and can reduce the risk associated with mining and energy investments depending on how investments in flow-through shares are structured. Under a flow-through share agreement, the investor enjoys limited liability, a specified share in any profits of the corporation, and a residual right in the property of the corporation on dissolution.

For mining and energy companies, flow-through shares can provide a less costly means of raising equity-based financing for eligible exploration, development, renewable energy, energy conservation, and energy efficiency activities. In addition, by permitting a widespread share issue, they allow access to a broad range of investors while minimizing the impact on corporate management and control. Although flow-through shares are available to all eligible mining and energy companies, the mechanism is intended to be of principal benefit to non-taxpaying junior companies, that is, companies that cannot immediately use income tax deductions and whose access to alternative sources of financing is limited.

What is the Policy Intent of Flow-Through Shares?

There is no explicit statement of policy intent relating to flow-through shares in Canadian federal budget documents. However, federal policy statements in respect of both tax and non-tax incentives for assisting mining and petroleum activities indicate that flow-through shares are used to support economic and social policy by: (1) encouraging additional exploration and development in Canada, (2) promoting equity investments in mining and petroleum companies, and (3) assisting junior (typically non-taxpaying) exploration companies whose access to internal sources of financing (that is, cash flow) may be limited.

The extension of the flow-through share provisions to certain renewable energy, energy conservation, and energy efficiency activities in the 1996 federal budget was made to improve the ability of renewable energy and energy conservation firms to access financing in the early stages of their operations, when they have little or no income to utilize the income tax deductions related to these expenses. The extension also helps level the playing field in the income tax treatment of renewable and non-renewable energy, and recognizes the importance of renewable energy and energy conservation to Canada's overall energy needs and environmental objectives.

What Factors Influence the Use of Flow-Through Shares?

Factors affecting the relative attractiveness of flow-through shares as a financing or investment vehicle can be grouped into three general categories. The first consists of design considerations relating to the flow-through share transaction. They include the specific terms of the flow-through share agreement, the types of eligible expenses to be incurred by companies and renounced to investors (because, for example, the tax value for exploration expenses is higher than for development expenses), and the income tax provisions that govern how eligible expenses can be renounced and bear on investor liability. The way in which investors choose to purchase flow-through shares will also affect the risk associated with the investment and the threshold for investor participation, and may influence how investors view their potential liability for third-party claims in respect of a company's activities.

The second category consists of fiscal influences, both federal and provincial, that affect the relative attractiveness of flow-through shares. These may be of general application or targeted specifically to flow-through shares. Income tax measures of general application include the definitions and deductibility of expenses eligible for flow-through shares, tax rates and surtaxes, and the treatment of capital gains realized on disposition of the corporate shares. Provincial governments have also sought to promote exploration and related activities within provincial boundaries by using a variety of income tax incentives that are targeted specifically to flow-through shares. Similarly, grant-based government programs influence, directly and indirectly, the use of flow-through shares.

Market conditions and investor preferences constitute a third category of factors that can affect the relative attractiveness of flow-through shares. The track record of the issuing company, including any previous experiences it may have had with flow-through shares, will affect its ability to raise funds using this equity-based financing mechanism. The general performance of mining or petroleum stocks will affect the amount of funding directed to that sector. Commodity price levels influence the attractiveness of alternative types of mineral deposits and energy sources as well as the degree of effort devoted to their discovery and development. Investor preferences pertaining to risk and expected rates of return, investments in particular types of mining or energy firms, and equity-based investments in these companies versus other types of investments help determine the overall level of funding available for flow-through shares.

How Popular Were Flow-Through Shares?

Although flow-through shares have been available since 1954, they became especially important, particularly as a financing vehicle for exploration by mining companies, in the second half of the 1980s. Their popularity during this period was the result of several factors, including favorable market conditions for mining (such as relatively high prices for gold and silver, and for mining stocks), the introduction of new fiscal incentives, improvements in the basic design of flow-through shares (such as the income tax changes in 1986 that limited investor liability), and increased participation in flow-through share transactions by large limited-partnership intermediaries.

The popularity of flow-through shares is evident from the fact that mining and petroleum companies raised $3.3 billion for exploration and development through this financing mechanism between 1987 and 1991. Of this total, $2.5 billion was for mining exploration; this amount represented about 60 percent of all funding raised for mining exploration over the period.

What Were the Central Evaluation Questions?

The Treasury Board of Canada (1992) provides guidelines for the conduct of program evaluations by the federal government. Under these guidelines, evaluations involve an empirically based analysis of the performance of programs in achieving their objectives. Program performance, in turn, is defined as the continued relevance, success, and cost-effectiveness of federal programs.

Relevance is the extent to which a program continues to be consistent with departmental and government-wide priorities and to address realistically an actual need. Success is the extent to which a program is effective in meeting its objectives, within budget and without significant unwanted outcomes.

Cost-effectiveness is the extent to which a program is the most appropriate and efficient means for achieving the objectives, relative to alternative design and delivery approaches, and is delivered in the most cost-effective manner.

In keeping with these guidelines, the central questions for the evaluation of flow-through shares conducted in 1992 and 1993 were the relevance, success (or effectiveness), and cost-effectiveness of flow-through shares in meeting their tax policy objectives for mining and oil and gas and considering the various design, fiscal, and market factors that affected their performance between 1983 and 1991. These aspects of performance are outlined in further detail below.

Relevance. To what extent did flow-through shares realistically address an actual need and to what extent were they consistent with government priorities between 1983 and 1991?

Budget papers and other government documents issued between 1983 and 1991 indicate that it was federal policy to help the mining and petroleum industries attract financing for exploration and development, to encourage risk-taking and equity investments in mining and petroleum companies, and to assist junior exploration companies. Flow-through shares were one means by which these policy objectives were pursued. Thus, to address relevance, the evaluation assessed the origins of the flow-through share mechanism and the extent to which flow-through shares offered an alternative to other financing mechanisms for exploration and development by mining and petroleum companies, and provided unique opportunities for achieving the government's policy objectives.

Effectiveness. To what extent were flow-through shares effective in meeting their policy objectives without unwanted outcomes between 1983 and 1991?

The effectiveness (or success) of flow-through shares was explored by examining: (1) amounts of flow-through share funding raised for exploration and development by mining and petroleum companies; (2) the degree to which this funding was spent on, and enhanced, exploration and development activities; (3) the role of partnership intermediaries in facilitating the flow-through share transaction; (4) the benefits flow-through shares provided to junior companies; (5) the capital-market sharing of the flow-through share premium between issuing companies and investors; and (6) whether investment decisions made by both issuing companies and investors were based more on economic merit than tax considerations.

Cost-Effectiveness. Were flow-through shares cost-effective in achieving their government policy objectives between 1983 and 1991, and to what extent were flow-through shares cost-effective relative to alternative financing mechanisms that could have achieved the same objectives?

Four aspects of the cost-effectiveness of flow-through shares were explored. Cost-effectiveness for the federal government was investigated by comparing the amount of incremental exploration spending generated by flow-through shares to federal tax expenditure estimates for exploration financed in this way. A perspective on cost-effectiveness for investors in flow-through shares was gained by analyzing rates of return realized by investors who purchased flow-through shares through certain broadly based limited partnerships (that is, those involved with over 40 issuing companies and having up to 14,000 investors). Cost-effectiveness for mining and petroleum companies was explored by considering the extent to which flow-through shares reduced the relative cost of raising equity-based financing for exploration and development. This was done by comparing marginal effective tax rates for alternative equity-based financing options—specifically, retained earnings, common shares, and flow-through shares. Marginal effective tax rates indicate the extent to which a new investment is encouraged by the tax system. The comparison indicated the relative cost-effectiveness of each form of financing and the relative ability of each to encourage exploration and development. Cost-effectiveness for society in general was considered by examining costs and rates of gold discovery in Canada since 1946.

Other than flow-through shares, no equity-based financing mechanism has ever existed in Canada that would afford the same opportunity for junior mining or petroleum companies to realize the tax value of new exploration and development expenditures before the companies become taxpaying. Consequently, it was not possible to compare empirically the cost-effectiveness of flow-through shares to alternative financing mechanisms designed to achieve the same policy objectives. Nevertheless, theoretical alternatives to flow-through shares were explored.

How Was the Evaluation Conducted?

A variety of methodologies were used to address the central evaluation questions. They included a historical review of tax policy and legislation for flow-through shares; a review of the literature on flow-through shares and tax-based financing alternatives; analyses of taxation, financial, and industry data; case studies of mining and petroleum firms and limited partnerships involved in flow-through share transactions; data questionnaires for mining and petroleum companies that issued flow-through shares; and economic and financial research into various aspects of the effectiveness and cost-effectiveness of flow-through shares.

Assistance in terms of data collection and analysis was provided by groups within Revenue Canada, the Ottawa Taxation Centre, and Natural Resources Canada. Databases on flow-through shares containing confidential taxpayer information were created at the Ottawa Taxation Centre as a direct consequence of the reporting requirements for companies and partnerships established under the Canadian Income Tax Act. Information on the administration of flow-through shares (that is, filing, audit, and reassessment) was obtained from Revenue Canada. Natural Resources Canada supplied publicly available statistics on exploration and development expenditures in the mining and petroleum industries, data on levels of assistance provided to the petroleum industry, information and analyses of flow-through shares in the case of the mining industry, and information on costs and rates of gold discoveries over time in Canada.

Three consultants from outside government were hired to provide specialized expertise on different aspects of the evaluation. One of the consultants conducted case studies involving direct and confidential contact with some of the mining and petroleum companies and limited partnerships that participated in flow-through share transactions between 1987 and mid-1992 (Peat Marwick Stevenson & Kellogg, 1993). A central focus of this work was estimating the incremental impacts and financing effectiveness of flow-through shares on exploration and development. Of interest, for example, were the views and expectations of the case study participants with respect to flow-through shares and the decision-making process they employed at the time they undertook the exploration or development financed by flow-through shares. This information was then used in conjunction with information from other sources (e.g., annual reports, prospectuses, and company and partnership data on flow-through shares from Revenue Canada files) to conduct independent analyses of the performance of flow-through shares in these respects.

The case studies were also used to collect information bearing on other aspects of this evaluation. One such aspect was to enhance understanding of how the exploration and development process for mining compared with that for oil and gas between 1987 and mid-1992. A broad range of issues raised by the case study participants concerning flow-through shares was also noted, and additional information was gathered on the structure of flow-through share agreements entered into between the issuing companies and their investors.

A second consultant (McKenzie, 1994) conducted economic research into: (1) the sharing of the flow-through share premium between issuing companies and investors, or, to state the matter differently, the effectiveness of flow-through shares in delivering the value of income tax deductions to issuing companies; and (2) how sharing of the premium affects the cost-effectiveness of flow-through shares in terms of their ability to reduce the relative cost of raising equity-based financing for exploration and development. In pursuing the former objective, consideration was given to the influence of tax provisions and capital markets on the flow-through share premium, and the purpose of flow-through shares. The latter objective was pursued by comparing marginal effective tax rates for alternative equity-based financing options and by drawing on the considerable literature that exists on this topic. The empirical portion of this study employed data on flow-through shares obtained directly from mining and petroleum companies. This information was gathered, by means of separate data questionnaires, from the same companies that volunteered to participate in the case studies.

A third consultant (Jog, 1994) considered the investment performance of flow-through shares—that is, their cost-effectiveness from the perspective of investors—by examining rates of return earned on flow-through shares purchased through certain broadly based limited partnerships between 1986 and

1990. The rationale for this work was that, although investors receive an immediate tax benefit from deducting eligible expenses that are renounced to them, rational investors must also weigh the risk inherent in the flow-through share investment against its return over the longer term.

What Did the Evaluation Find?

The evaluation found that, between 1983 and 1991, flow-through shares were generally relevant, effective, and cost-effective in meeting the federal government's policy objectives of encouraging exploration in Canada, stimulating equity-based investments in mining and petroleum companies, and assisting junior exploration companies.

Relevance. Flow-through shares were consistent with government priorities between 1983 and 1991, and addressed a need identified by industry. Flow-through shares were one means by which the federal government pursued its policy objectives of stimulating exploration and development, encouraging risk-taking and equity investments in mining and petroleum companies, and assisting junior exploration companies. Flow-through shares help to stimulate exploration and development by, in essence, allowing mining and petroleum companies to transfer otherwise unusable or unused tax deductions relating to these investments to investors in exchange for a premium over the market price of the company's common shares.

Flow-through shares occupy a unique place among the various specialized financing alternatives available to facilitate investments in exploration and development by mining and petroleum companies. Four such alternatives were considered, each possessing distinct characteristics: joint ventures, joint exploration corporations, partnerships, and limited partnerships. These financing options allow investors to claim income tax deductions for exploration and development expenses in the manner most suitable to their particular circumstances and preferences. The flow-through share mechanism stands in marked contrast to each of these financing alternatives, possessing a unique combination of features that rendered it the most readily accessible financing structure, and resulted in its relatively widespread commercial application in the second half of the 1980s.

The flow-through share financing mechanism responded to a need identified by mining and petroleum companies. It was conceived by them after exploration and development expenditures became fully deductible in calculating income tax in 1947. The mechanism allowed junior companies to obtain the funding or expertise necessary to explore and develop promising mineral or petroleum prospects. It provided a practical and efficient commercial forum for recognizing and accommodating the differing contributions of the issuing company and its investors, and facilitated financing for exploration and development by allowing investors to realize, directly and immediately, the tax value associated with expenditures on exploration and development. This expenses-for-shares transaction was subsequently recognized in income tax legislation for the 1954 taxation year, at which time certain conditions were introduced to define its scope and operation.

Effectiveness. Evaluation findings were mixed in regard to the effectiveness of flow-through shares in achieving its objectives between 1983 and 1991. On the positive side, flow-through shares raised a substantial amount of equity-based financing for exploration and development (particularly for mining exploration and for gold exploration); were the dominant means by which funding was raised for mining exploration; resulted in significant incremental spending on mining and petroleum exploration and significant incremental exploration drilling activity; benefited the economies of Alberta, British Columbia, Ontario, and Quebec; and assisted non-taxpaying junior exploration companies.

However, incremental exploration activity generated by flow-through shares was not particularly high, inflated exploration drilling costs were experienced in the mining industry, and there was little evidence that the incremental exploration spending and activity resulted in incremental discoveries attributable to this financing mechanism. Flow-through shares were also often tax-motivated investments that focused on more valuable exploration write-offs and were characterized by relatively rapid spending by issuing companies and share disposition by investors. The effectiveness of flow-through shares in raising financing was found to depend crucially on price levels for minerals and petroleum (especially world prices for gold and silver), general economic conditions (such as the 1990 economic recession), the economic prospects of the issuing company, the fiscal treatment of the exploration and development expenditures renounced to investors, and the bargaining power of investors relative to the issuing companies.

Levels of Flow-Through Share Financing. Flow-through shares were used to raise $3.3 billion for exploration and development by mining and petroleum companies between 1987 and 1991. Of this amount: 93 percent ($3.0 billion) was for exploration; and 75 percent ($2.5 billion) was for mining exploration.

Renunciations of mining exploration expenses, in 1991 dollars, rose from $45 million in 1983 to a peak of $1.1 billion in 1987 due to the combined effects of: (1) improvements to the design of flow-through shares (such as the 1986 federal budget change that limited investor liability and the increased involvement of broadly based limited partnerships in the transaction); (2) new fiscal incentives (such as the mining exploration depletion allowance—a bonus deduction for "grass-roots" mining exploration available between April 1983 and December 1989—and the general lifetime capital gains exemption for individuals—an income tax incentive for certain equity investments available between January 1985 and February 1994 that provided an income tax exemption of up to $100,000 of cumulative capital gains); and (3) favorable market conditions for mining (such as relatively high prices for gold and silver and for mining stocks).

The attractiveness of flow-through shares was significantly reduced after 1987 due to a deterioration in market conditions (such as falling commodity and share prices for gold and silver, and the 1990 economic recession) and the 1987 income tax reform in Canada, which reduced the tax-advantaged status of flow-through shares (for example, by reducing personal income tax rates and, therefore, the value of income tax deductions, by increasing the capital gains inclusion rate and by phasing out the mining exploration depletion allowance). Nevertheless, the $65 million of mining exploration expenses renounced in 1991 was almost 50 percent higher than the $45 million (in 1991 dollars) renounced in 1983.

A total of 2,035 companies issued flow-through shares between 1987 and 1991. Mining companies composed 75 percent of these companies and issued flow-through shares almost exclusively (99.8 percent of the funding raised) to finance exploration. A disproportionately small number of issuing companies made the majority of renunciations to investors (for example, 4 percent of companies renounced amounts in excess of $10 million and accounted for 37 percent of renunciations between 1987 and 1991) and the general trend after 1987 was for fewer companies to renounce smaller amounts of both exploration and development expenses.

Due to the location of mineral deposits and petroleum reserves in Canada, flow-through shares had important regional impacts. Ontario, British Columbia, and Quebec were the principal beneficiaries in the case of mining; Alberta was the principal beneficiary in the case of oil and gas. Of the companies that issued flow-through shares between 1987 and 1991, 98 percent were located in British Columbia, Alberta, Ontario, and Quebec, with the provinces ranked in that order, and these companies accounted for 95 percent of the $3.3 billion renounced over this period. However, this provincial ranking was reversed in terms of the average amount renounced per company.

Impacts on Exploration and Development. The pattern of mining exploration expenditures from 1983 to 1991 mirrors the pattern of renunciations of mining exploration expenses through flow-through shares. Levels of mining exploration expenditures increased generally from 1983, peaked in 1987 and 1988, and fell thereafter. After 1986, annual renunciations of mining exploration expenses averaged 60 cents per dollar of mining exploration and ranged from a high of 82 cents per dollar in 1988 to a low of 17 cents per dollar in 1991. Thus, flow-through shares played a significant role in financing mining exploration, but their importance declined precipitously after 1988.

Over the period 1983 to 1991, the annual average amount of exploration expenditures in the petroleum industry was about four times higher than in the mining industry. The pattern of petroleum exploration expenditures was also markedly different from the pattern of mining exploration expenditures. Petroleum exploration spending peaked in 1984 and 1985 and declined sharply thereafter. Renunciations of petroleum exploration expenses accounted for a relatively constant annual average of only 6 cents per dollar of petroleum exploration. Evidence suggested that world oil price levels and grant-based government incentives were more important factors influencing petroleum exploration spending than the availability of flow-through share financing.

Renunciations of development expenses and property acquisition costs were relatively insignificant from 1987 to 1991, and flow-through shares were not an important source of financing for either of these purposes.

Incremental mining exploration expenditures attributable to flow-through shares are estimated at 49 percent of all exploration spending between 1987 and 1991 by the mining companies that participated in the case studies. Incrementality for petroleum exploration expenditures equaled 30 percent of all exploration spending by the petroleum companies in the sample.

There was considerable evidence of "overheating" in the mining industry, in terms of increased drilling costs and declines in project quality, as companies sought to make tax deductions for exploration and development expenditures available to investors in the same taxation year in which the flow-through share funding was raised. Due to this overheating, physical incrementality (that is, incremental drilling activity) for mining exploration was estimated to be 11 percentage points lower than incremental mining exploration spending. In contrast, there was no evidence that the petroleum industry was affected by overheating. A key reason for this difference may have been significant excess capacity in the petroleum industry caused by the adverse effects of the decline in world oil prices in 1986.

Although empirical estimates of incremental discoveries could not be generated, anecdotal evidence suggests that some incremental discoveries were directly attributable to flow-through shares. Furthermore, information obtained through exploration financed by flow-through shares may lead to incremental discoveries in the future.

Partnership Intermediaries. Flow-through shares were facilitated significantly by the participation of partnerships, particularly limited partnerships, in the transaction. A total of 263 partnerships were involved in flow-through share agreements between 1987 and 1991. These partnerships were the primary means by which flow-through shares were issued, accounting for 61 percent ($2.0 billion) of renunciations over the period, and raised funds almost entirely for exploration and primarily for mining. In contrast, direct issuance to investors was the dominant mode for all categories of expenses renounced by petroleum companies. Mining companies that employed both partnership intermediaries and direct issuance accounted for the largest amount of renunciations from 1987 to 1991. Most petroleum companies used only direct issuance.

Most renunciations by means of partnership intermediaries occurred in 1987 and 1988, although renunciations in this manner remained high in proportion to total renunciations (over 50 percent) between 1987 and 1990. The number of partnerships, companies renouncing to partnerships, and amounts renounced to partnerships declined significantly each year after 1987. Partnerships that were the most successful in raising flow-through share financing also achieved the greatest amount of asset diversification and risk reduction by entering into agreements with large numbers of companies. The majority of expenses were renounced to a disproportionately small number of partnerships which included the broadly based limited partnerships. For example, 7 percent of partnerships received renunciations in excess of $25 million each and collectively accounted for 65 percent of renunciations between 1987 and 1991.

Junior Exploration Companies. Junior mining companies benefited significantly from flow-through shares. Their share of mining exploration expenditures in Canada more than tripled from 15 percent in 1983 to over 51 percent in 1987, but fell after 1988 to 21 percent in 1991. The bulk of this exploration spending was financed by flow-through shares. Flow-through shares were also important to junior petroleum companies; their share of petroleum exploration spending in Canada increased by 75 percent between 1983 and 1987 and remained relatively stable to 1991. Due to the participation of limited partnerships, flow-through share funding for junior companies could also be raised with relative ease, although these companies often received only a small premium on their shares.

Premiums and Sharing. The maximum premium over the price of a common share that a flow-through share investor would be willing to pay equals the value, to that investor, of the tax deductions and incentives for exploration or development. Income tax provisions affecting the maximum premium include personal income tax rates, rates of deductibility for renounced expenses, the capital gains inclusion rate, and the availability of the lifetime capital gains exemption.

Even in a well-functioning capital market, however, the observed price of flow-through shares will invariably reflect a premium—the observed premium—that is less than the maximum premium. And in paying a premium that is less than the maximum, investors effectively share in the tax benefits of the flow-through shares with the issuing firm. The specific factors that may lead to this outcome include tax-induced investor surplus, incremental liquidity risk, incremental transaction costs, and the influence of limited-partnership intermediaries.

Tax-induced investor surplus arises if issuing firms fail to attract investors in the highest marginal tax bracket. Incremental liquidity risk may arise because flow-through share agreements usually do not require immediate delivery of the underlying common share to investors, with the result that an investor who has committed funds to flow-through shares normally cannot sell the shares until the holding period has expired. Incremental transaction costs are costs associated with issuing flow-through shares that exceed the costs of financing exploration or development through the issuance of common shares. Larger limited partnerships typically offered higher premiums to senior companies because of the attractiveness of their shares relative to the shares of junior companies and to mining companies because of the attractiveness of fiscal incentives for mining exploration.

Other research papers model the pricing of flow-through shares relative to the pricing of common shares and take account of the income tax provisions of the issuing companies and the investors. These papers propose that sharing of the flow-through share premium between issuing companies and investors can be used to assess the relative effectiveness of flow-through shares as a mechanism for delivering the value of tax benefits to issuing companies; specifically, they argue that sharing is evidence of ineffectiveness. Henin and Ryan (1987), Boadway and McKenzie (1989) and Jenkins (1987, 1990) develop theoretical pricing equations and consider the relative effectiveness of flow-through shares as a mechanism for delivering the value of income tax deductions to issuing firms. Except for Jenkins, however, none of the papers provide empirical evidence. Nor do any of them acknowledge that the sharing of premium between the investors and the issuing company occurs in well-functioning capital markets and that this sharing has important implications for assessing effectiveness. Finally, none of the papers considers the cost-effectiveness of flow-through shares as a means of encouraging new investment or as an investment vehicle.

Research undertaken for the evaluation provided new insights into the effectiveness of mechanisms of this type and showed that the existence of sharing does not mean that flow-through shares are ineffective. Indeed, this research shows that the benchmark used by others to assess the effectiveness of flow-through shares may not be appropriate. Furthermore, it is argued that an appropriate alternative benchmark for assessing the effectiveness of flow-through shares is the financing of new exploration and development through new equity issuance in capital markets. This alternative would result in a similar sharing of the tax benefits between the investors and the firm. The research also indicates that flow-through shares are most effective as a delivery mechanism when firms are non-taxpaying and investors are subject to the lowest tax rate and cannot access the lifetime capital gains exemption. (Jog, Lenjosek, and McKenzie, 1996) also consider the matter of flow-through shares as a tax-benefit delivery mechanism. Specifically, they investigate how and why the flow-through share premium is shared between issuing companies and investors and the significance of this sharing in terms of the effectiveness of flow-through shares. They also explore the cost-effectiveness of flow-through shares from the perspectives of issuing companies and investors.)

The Users of Flow-Through Shares. Corporate income tax data for 1987 to 1990 indicated that a "typical" issuing company was a non-taxpaying Canadian public corporation based in either British Columbia, Alberta, Ontario, or Quebec. However, a marked distinction existed between mining and petroleum companies. Mining companies were more likely to be non-taxpaying public corporations based in either British Columbia, Ontario, or Quebec. Petroleum companies were more likely to be taxpaying Canadian-controlled private corporations either based in Alberta or with a multi-jurisdictional base of operations. These differences reflect both the differing nature of the two industries and the geographical location of mineral and petroleum resources in Canada.

Based on personal income tax data for 1989 and 1990, a "typical" flow-through share investor can be described as a married male in his forties who resides in Quebec or Ontario, is an employee, and is in the top income tax bracket. However, the profile of "aggressive" investors, in terms of the proportion of their total income spent on flow-through shares, is quite different. Such investors were more likely to be married females; under 30 years of age; residents of either the Yukon, Saskatchewan, Manitoba, or New Brunswick; medical doctors or dentists; and subject to the lowest income tax rates.

Underlying Investment Rationale. In considering a potential investment in flow-through shares, an investor would be interested in both its tax features and its longer-term investment potential. However, evidence strongly suggests that the issuance of flow-through shares between 1983 and 1991 was based more on tax considerations than the economic merit of the underlying mining or petroleum activity. Mutual fund managers reported that investors were almost solely interested in the tax write-offs available from flow-through shares.

It was also found that investors usually did not purchase flow-through shares until the end of any given year, at which time they were more aware of their tax situations. To provide for a deduction in the same calendar year, mining and petroleum companies generally sought to incur and renounce expenditures (especially exploration expenditures, which are more valuable for tax purposes) in that year or within the first 60 days of the subsequent calendar year. As noted above, there was considerable evidence that this behavior led to overheating in the mining industry, but not in the petroleum industry.

Another indication of tax-motivated investments was the fundamental mismatch between the investment horizons of investors and issuing companies. Investors tended to sell their shares at the earliest opportunity, whereas companies, particularly junior explorers, were more interested in a longer-term source of funds. The enormous downward pressure on share prices exerted by this investor behavior presented substantial problems for issuing companies that had not yet attained some measure of exploration success. Although substantial quantities of gold were discovered between 1983 and 1990 relative to the period from 1946 to 1979, the small size of the deposits suggests that exploration effort may have been concentrated on already-known and less-promising mineral deposits in order to meet the needs of flow-through share investors within a relatively short time frame.

Cost-Effectiveness. As in the case of effectiveness, evaluation findings in respect of the cost-effectiveness of flow-through shares were mixed. On one hand, flow-through shares resulted in substantially more incremental exploration spending than federal tax revenues foregone. Economic research indicated that they are the most cost-effective equity-based financing option for non-taxpaying exploration companies and empirical evidence revealed that they provided a significant incentive for exploration by non-taxpaying firms. On the other hand, flow-through shares performed poorly as equity investments in mining and petroleum.

Incremental Spending Per Dollar of Federal Tax Expenditure. Because flow-through shares allow investors to access income tax deductions for exploration and development more quickly than the companies that issue them, they result in a tax cost to government. The net federal tax cost of mining and petroleum exploration financed by flow-through shares was estimated at $563 million for the period 1987 to 1991; the annual amount of this tax expenditure declined dramatically from $283 million in 1987 to $14 million in 1991 (Department of Finance Canada, 1994, pp. 167–169). Over 80 percent of the federal tax expenditures over this period was in respect of mining. Between 1987 and 1991, each dollar of federal tax expenditure resulted in incremental expenditures of, on average, $3 in the case of mining exploration and $2 in the case of petroleum exploration.

Cost-Effectiveness for Investors. Conclusions about the cost-effectiveness of flow-through shares from an investor's viewpoint were mixed. An analysis of the rates of return earned by investors in certain broadly based limited partnerships over the period 1986 through 1990 revealed that the investment performance of flow-through shares was not very attractive. The pricing of flow-through shares may have favored the investor in 1986, but in later years it favored the issuing firms or the flow-through share partnerships. If there were no incremental transaction costs associated with issuing flow-through shares, then most of the tax benefits were captured by issuing firms. Moreover, these benefits accrued to firms whose shares performed relatively worse than did an average share in the corresponding subindustry.

Cost-Effectiveness for Issuing Companies. The comparison of marginal effective tax rates for retained earnings, common shares, and flow-through shares (based both on the maximum premium and the observed premium) indicated that flow-through shares can be cost-effective for issuing firms and provide significant encouragement to exploration. The actual level of incentive depends on the extent of capital-market sharing of the flow-through share premium between issuing companies and investors, corporate and personal income tax provisions, and the opportunity cost to firms of forgone tax deductions. The maximum premium has its counterpart in the theoretical marginal effective tax rate for flow-through shares; the observed premium, in the empirical marginal effective tax rate.

Marginal effective tax rates for exploration financed by flow-through shares are lowest: (1) when issuing firms receive the maximum premium possible from their investors, and (2) for non-taxpaying firms. For non-taxpaying firms, flow-through shares yield lower (theoretical) marginal effective tax rates than do either retained earnings or common shares, a result that implies that flow-through shares are the most cost-effective of the three financing options. However, theoretical marginal effective tax rates for taxpaying firms can be negative and less than marginal effective tax rates for common shares. This result implies that flow-through shares can offer encouragement even to taxpaying firms to increase their exploration efforts. Generally, however, retained earnings are the most cost-effective method of financing exploration for taxpaying firms.

If the premium received by issuing firms is less than the maximum premium, the marginal effective tax rate for flow-through shares increases. The actual cost-effectiveness of flow-through shares can be determined only through empirical investigation. Calculations of illustrative empirical marginal effective tax rates on the basis of observed premiums reinforced the conclusion that flow-through shares provided a significant incentive for exploration by non-taxpaying firms in spite of the sharing of the premium between the issuing company and its investors. Furthermore, the incentive for non-taxpaying firms to finance exploration by issuing flow-through shares was much the same as the incentive for a taxpaying firm in a similar situation to finance exploration out of its retained earnings. Incentive grants and bonus deductions were found to increase cost-effectiveness and promote exploration by reducing marginal effective tax rates regardless of the financing option employed.

Cost-Effectiveness for Society. In terms of the overall benefit to the Canadian economy, there were substantial discoveries of smaller gold deposits between 1983 and 1990 relative to earlier periods, but they have not yet been fully appraised due to unfavorable market conditions. In addition, due in part to overheating, the unit cost of discoveries between 1985 and 1990 was about 2.5 times as high as during typical periods. The ratio of the value of gold discoveries to the cost of exploration was about one-half the ratio for typical periods. Taken together, these findings suggest that flow-through share financed exploration between 1983 and 1990 may not have been as cost-effective as exploration efforts in earlier periods.

Summary

The evaluation employed a variety of methodologies to assess the performance of flow-through shares between 1983 and 1991. Each of the methodologies contributed information necessary for addressing this issue. The central evaluation questions of relevance, effectiveness, and cost-effectiveness were pursued by combining information from each of the individual sources. The overall finding was that flow-through shares were generally relevant, effective, and cost-effective in meeting the federal government's policy objectives of encouraging exploration in Canada, stimulating equity-based investments in mining and petroleum companies, and assisting junior exploration companies.

Structural, fiscal, and economic factors combined to influence the level, and the share, of exploration spending financed by flow-through shares. Between 1983 and 1987, these factors exerted a positive influence; between 1988 and 1991, a negative influence. The evaluation did not separately identify the quantitative impact of individual factors affecting flow-through shares and exploration activities.

Large amounts of equity-based financing for exploration were raised by flow-through shares between 1983 and 1991, so the mechanism was effective in this sense. However, the effectiveness of flow-through shares in generating incremental mining and petroleum exploration was reduced due to, for example, disproportionate increases in gold exploration activity, overheating (that is, inflated drilling costs) in mining exploration, downward pressure being exerted by large limited partnerships on the premium received by junior companies, and tax-motivated flow-through share investments during the mid-1980s. Within the much less favorable investment climate that existed in 1991, the motivation for investing in flow-through shares shifted toward their underlying investment potential as opposed to their tax features. Flow-through share agreements also began to move beyond their preoccupation with the search for gold to encompass a more balanced portfolio of minerals.

Empirical evidence indicates that the tax benefits of flow-through shares were shared between investors and issuing companies and that this sharing tended to vary inversely with firm size due, in part, to the influence of the limited partnerships. In addition, empirical evidence reveals that flow-through shares performed very poorly when compared to an equity investment in an index of mining and petroleum stocks between 1986 and 1990. This poor investment performance directly affected the demand for flow-through shares as well, both by individual investors and by limited partnerships. Diminished investor interest and involvement by limited partnerships compromised the effectiveness of flow-through shares in assisting junior companies and in financing exploration spending.

Flow-through shares were a cost-effective means to finance exploration in that they induced incremental exploration spending in excess of federal tax expenditures, but the same factors that reduced their effectiveness also reduced their cost-effectiveness. Regardless, flow-through shares were a cost-effective financing mechanism for non-taxpaying companies throughout the period and as effective as any possible equity-based financing alternative designed to achieve the same objectives.

References

Boadway, R., and McKenzie, K. "The Treatment of Resource Industries in the 1987 Federal Tax Reform." In Jack Mintz and John Whalley (eds.), The Economic Impacts of Tax Reform. Toronto: Canadian Tax Foundation, 1989. (Canadian Tax Paper No. 84)

Department of Finance Canada. Flow-Through Shares: An Evaluation Report. Oct. 1994.

Department of Finance Canada. Budget Plan. Mar. 6, 1996.

Henin, C., and Ryan, P. J. "Structuring the Flow-Through Share Offer." Proceedings of the Administrative Sciences Association of Canada, 1987.

Jenkins, G. P. "Cost-Effectiveness of After-Tax Financing: Flow-Through Shares in Canada." Economic Council of Canada, Discussion Paper No. 327. June 1987.

Jenkins, G. P. "Tax Shelter Finance: How Efficient Is It?" Canadian Tax Journal, Mar./Apr. 1990, 38 (2)

Jog, V. J. "Cost-Effectiveness for Investors." In Department of Finance Canada, Flow-Through Shares: An Evaluation Report, pp. 143–158. Oct. 1994..

Jog, V. M., Lenjosek, G. J., and McKenzie, K. J. "Flow-Through Shares: Premium Sharing and Cost-Effectiveness." Canadian Tax Journal, Oct. 1996, 44 (4).

McKenzie, K. J. The Effectiveness of Flow Through Shares. Report prepared for the Department of Finance, Canada, Mar. 1994.

Peat Marwick Stevenson & Kellogg Management Consultants. Flow-Through Share Case Studies. Report prepared for the Department of Finance Canada, Dec. 1993.

Treasury Board of Canada. Evaluation and Audit Manual for the Government of Canada. Jan. 1992.

GORDON J. LENJOSEK *is manager of R&D policy and evaluation in the Tax Policy Branch of the Department of Finance Canada.*

What does the work on tax expenditures over the last decade imply about the better design of evaluations in this area? The tax expenditure evaluations are compared against a simple but sturdy general framework for conducting results evaluations that looks at target populations; the treatment, program, or policy; the response variable; how relative effects are estimated; and what happens when no effects are discovered.

Taxes, Tax Expenditures, and Evaluation—Pleasing and Otherwise

Robert F. Boruch

"To tax and to please, no more than to love and be wise, is not given to men." So said Edmund Burke in 1794 in a speech that reflected his ambivalence about the colonies' fiscal relations with Britain—not to speak of his love life. Now, he might have added: "But to create tax expenditures does please some men, is given, and may also be in the nation's interest."

Roughly speaking, the phrase *tax expenditures* here refers to loss incurred by government when it enacts special exemptions to an ordinary tax. It embodies the idea that the public and its vicar, government, forgo an income and, in effect, spend when exceptions to a tax rule are made.

This chapter reviews the remarkable set of papers on tax expenditures in this issue of *New Directions for Evaluation*. Their authors, whose work was invited and edited by Patrick Grasso and Lois-ellin Datta, are identified below. Other material that is exploited in what follows includes an underused volume issued by the National Academy of Sciences (Roth, Scholz, and Witte, 1989) and studies generated by the U.S. Internal Revenue Service and the U.S. General Accounting Office.

The review has one major objective: exploring what the work on tax expenditures over the last decade implies about the better design of evaluations in this arena. The framework used to arrange thinking about this topic is pedestrian but sturdy. It covers major elements of evaluation, identified by the interrogatory topic headings in what follows. Theory of how interventions are supposed to work drives many evaluative choices, and this too is considered below.

What Is the Target Population?

Generally, evaluators make strenuous efforts to determine who is supposed to be served by the policy or program at issue. The task is apropos here. More interestingly, tax expenditure work highlights another kind of population, notably the totality of tax expenditure plans or programs. More subtly, we must confront peculiar differences in the way the target population is defined and how this may change over decades.

Consider first the ordinary issue of who is served. Expenditure provisions may affect relevant taxpayers directly, as with exemptions for children or mortgages. Or, they may affect corporations directly, as with exemptions for spending on research and development. There are, of course, indirect services. That is, something also happens to family members when a child exemption is enacted, as it does to a corporation's staff, customers, or competitors when a research and development exemption is used.

The target populations, in principle, may be easily specifiable, be they units, individuals, or corporations. But a feature of the tax expenditure system that is common in other evaluative settings puts a probabilistic constraint on this. In particular, the members of the actual population (in contrast to the target population) are those who: (a) know about the exemption, (b) understand it, (c) are in a position to employ it, and (d) are willing to employ it. For example, virtually all taxpayers with children arguably are aware of child exemptions and understand them, satisfying conditions (a) and (b). Only those with children can employ it, satisfying condition (c). Entities may or may not know about certain tax provisions and understand them; this depends heavily on tax counsel. Moreover, they may not be able to exploit the provision. And if they are able, they may be unwilling. As Davie suggested in Chapter One, a corporation may prefer the exemption for charitable donations to public television over another exemption for advertising on account of the increased prestige that the former action entails.

Earlier in this section, we recognized that the tax expenditures work invited thinking about a different kind of target population: the population of expenditure programs. In effect, this is a population of treatments rather than a target population of service recipients. Thinking about such populations is not a familiar exercise for many evaluators. But some policy analysts do it, along with to a small coterie of evaluators who do chores in the policy arena. Let us examine this topic under a conventional evaluation rubric: the treatment.

What Is the Treatment, Program, or Policy?

In some respects, a distinctive feature of tax expenditures work is that the provisions for expenditures constitute a target population of "treatments" or "programs" in the evaluator's vernacular. To complicate matters, each of these treatments is tied to a different population of those who are serviced, e.g., child exemptions for a family versus research and development exemptions for a corporation. Suppose we focus first on these treatments and their variety, and how we might arrange thinking about these.

The variety in the kinds of tax expenditure provisions appears great. Provisions may be customary or traditional, as in exemptions for children and mortgages or for advertising. They may involve plausible theory of what might happen, as in the case of certain corporate provisions, or implausible theory. They may involve language or conditions that must be read and understood carefully, or language or conditions that are simple. They may engage state or local governments, corporations that are for profit and otherwise, and individuals and families whose circumstances are complicated.

This treatment population may also be defined institutionally in different ways. As mentioned in Chapter One, the Congress's Joint Committee on Taxation defines such treatments as provisions that arguably result in losses of $100 million over five years. On the other hand, the United States Treasury Department denominates a tax expenditure in terms of a year and a $5 million loss to government.

One implication for evaluators is that they, like colleagues in the policy arena, have to learn how to recognize this numerousness and the qualitative and quantitative variations. For the sampling statistician who is interested in a national characterization of tax expenditures, these various kinds are the raw material for choosing units of sampling and constructing sample strata, perhaps building different strata systems to help portray expenditures differently. For the evaluator with interests in impact, these kinds may be stratified and then sampled to use as a basis for estimating relative differences among them in producing fiscal returns and losses, or in changing behavior of their targets.

A feature that is a bit unusual here relative to other evaluation contexts is the wide time frame for treatments. For instance, to employ the low-income housing tax credit, the required compliance period is fifteen years for those who wish to receive the credit (see Chapter Three). Presumably, a full-blown evaluation study might run well over fifteen years to gauge the cumulative effects of the treatment. Complicating how the evaluator may think about time frame is the fact that expenditure programs may be actually employed well after the point that enabling legislation is passed. Canadian law on equity investments in mining and engineering companies was enacted in 1954, for example. But it was not until the 1980s that economic conditions, the price of gold among others, invited corporate attention to the tax incentives (see Chapter Seven).

Further complicating the choice of time frame is the fact that a legislature, the U.S. Congress for instance, changes relevant law at times, as indeed it must. For instance, each major tax reform made in 1986, 1990, and 1993, according to Hill, Hotz, and Scholz in Chapter Two, revised tax rules credit for poor working families. An evaluator, working after the fact on the impact of such credit, must choose time frames for a baseline and for deployment of the program including its escalation or decline. This forces the evaluator to be reactionary, to do postmortems. It does not always permit the evaluator to understand in advance what the proper time frame for evaluation may be, to be proactive rather than reactive. Unless the evaluation is incorporated into legislation at each change in law the evaluator becomes, in Florence Nightingale's phrase, " . . . a shuttlecock between two battledores." A shuttlecock can serve a passive function. A prospective evaluation can do far more, to judge from the Salk vaccine's randomized trials, High/Scope and Tennessee's class size experiments (Finn and Achilles, 1990), and others.

For some areas of evaluation, massive variety in treatments and uncertain time frames are not uncommon. In education, for instance, the U.S. Department of Education Planning and Evaluation Service(USDE/PES) has managed to bring more order to the way we look at certain federally funded programs in adult literacy, Chapter I, prison education, and other areas. Designing the educational evaluations is easier for the USDE, one may argue, because rudimentary theory of education achievement is explicit. The theory of how tax expenditure provisions are supposed to work is sometimes less explicit or at least very complicated. This brings us to the next topic.

What Is the Response Variable?

Evaluators are used to being told that an intervention is supposed to affect dozens of different outcomes. In this respect, the tax expenditures arena is not different from education, health services, and criminal justice. The more sophisticated evaluators are able to cull the list with discretion and scientific sense. The evaluator's job, at times, is to understand which are most important. It is to understand which variables ought to be put at lower priority because their theoretical relevance to the program is weak.

In the tax expenditures arena, choosing outcome variables is sometimes easy. Estimated revenue that may be lost or gained by a government tax agency is such a variable. It is natural if one expects a loss, for example, as a direct consequence of allowing tax credits for research and development.

However, as in evaluations of programs in literacy, crime prevention, and supported housing, among others, choosing outcome variables and their method of measurement can be complicated. For instance, a major goal of tax expenditures is often to change certain behaviors. The goal may be ostensible or real, but is a goal. More importantly, the goal, its reflection in some outcome variable, and the particular tax expenditure are linked by theory. However ill-framed the theory might be, it usually must be made explicit by the evaluator so as to make a sensible choice about what to measure. This reiteration of a lesson is implicit in the papers at hand.

For example, tuition tax credits for post-secondary education are based on a theory, to judge from Davie's description in Chapter One, that credit will foster more college attendance by high school graduates and those seeking to enhance their employment-related abilities. Any assessment of the credit's consequences would have to exploit data on college or course enrollment and perhaps completion rates.

Theories are often unclear, however. Consider, for instance, that the theory driving tax credits for no-interest loans to school districts is far from clear. How and why corporate entities or school systems are supposed to act in this quarter, at what stage, in the face of what kind of competition and other priorities, and with what level of high-road perspective has not been worked out, and might never be. How any such theory relates to other theories of how human behavior changes is not obvious.

Choosing a variable does not mean it can be observed or measured, of course. Tax expenditure evaluations are distinctive in that they may rely on access to individual or corporate tax returns, supplemented by other data. Eligibility for Earned Income Tax Credit, for instance, appears partly determinable from household tax returns, although the evaluator may also depend on the Survey of Program Participation (see Chapter Two). Tax returns have been used in studies of Low-Income Housing Tax Credit (see Wallace, Chapter Three) and Employee Stock Ownership Plans (see Hanford, Chapter Four); these also being supplemented by independent surveys or case studies.

Most important, access to tax returns is restricted. The IRS may conduct analyses of tax expenditures or the U.S. General Accounting Office (GAO) may do so, given each agency's statutory authority to review such microrecords. But civilian researchers are generally shut out from direct access. Getting analyses done by the IRS then depends on the IRS's capacity and willingness to cooperate with independent researchers. The limited capacity has apparently been an obstacle to some well-designed evaluations in the employment and training arena, although the IRS has been conscientious in meeting its obligations both to preserve privacy and to make data as useful as possible (Duncan, Jabine, and de Wolfe, 1993). None of the papers in this volume explores the problems engendered by privacy statute or the feasibility and desirability of enlarging the IRS's ability to do analyses specified by external evaluators or to permit external analyses. The topic deserves more attention if indeed one believes that talent apart from the GAO, IRS, and their contractors can refresh evaluations of tax expenditure systems.

How Do We Estimate Relative Effects?

For the evaluator, the fundamental problems in estimating effect are to: (a) determine what happens when an intervention is deployed, (b) determine or estimate what would have happened if the intervention had not been deployed, and (c) compare these two, while simultaneously (d) recognizing that chance and events or government action apart from the intervention might influence a difference.

Controlled randomized experiments are a sturdy device for doing all this, especially when the theory of how the program is supposed to work is frail. In fact, such experiments have been run in some tax arenas. A small but unreplicated classic is the work by Schwartz and Orleans (1967) on how to motivate better compliance among taxpayers. The treatments included appeals to moral conscience, threats of legal action, and threats of social embarrassment. (The latter seemed to have worked best for the most affluent; the moral approach worked best for the least affluent.) Workmanly experiments by Perng (1985) helped the IRS to understand how various kinds of forms are useful or useless at reminding people to pay their taxes. And, of course, the IRS's random audits have been, in effect, randomized experiments on how auditing influences subsequent taxpayer compliance (Roth, Scholz, and Witte, 1989).

Components of systems may be testable even when experiments on a large legal system, such as the tax expenditures, are not. Witness the Corsi and Hurley (1979) field experiments on the use of telephone hearings versus in-person hearings in administrative law cases. The communication setting was an important component of the entire system.

As the editors of this issue suggested, the negative income tax experiments of the 1970s can be regarded as controlled studies on one kind of tax expenditures system. Individuals in the low-income levels within the treated group were provided with a partial tax reimbursement. The reimbursement amount depended on income level and family size. Depending on the level, individuals may also have received a grant, beyond the reimbursement, to bring them to the financial support threshold level set as a minimum. Control group members also were taxed but received no reimbursement; they would have received grants to bring them to the support level. The tax reimbursement in the Seattle and Denver Income Maintenance (SIME/DIME) experiments, for instance, can be regarded as a tax expenditure. For a summary of SIME/DIME, see Robins, Spiegelman, Weiner, and Bell, 1980.

Examples of this sort are suggestive in the sense that they illustrate the feasibility of controlled experiments in certain law-related arenas and their value. They are not proof of feasibility, of course. But they invite us to consider whether randomized controlled tests on tax expenditures are worth doing and how feasible they might be. For example, mandating experiments that test how people might be better informed about tax expenditure provisions seems feasible. After all, information is a manipulable variable, yet the information on such matters is not always and quickly available to the taxpayer. Moreover, the Treasury and IRS have a statutory authority to improve administration. This effort may include tests of innovative administrative approaches.

Rather more ambition seems justified in view of the character of tax expenditures. We can conceive of controlled experiments that use mixtures of expenditure provisions as the treatments, *mixture* being defined as when a provision kicks in, whether it is staged over one, two or five years, and which entities are eligible. Such experiments require enormous control and sophistication to judge from analogues in industrial chemistry or pharmaceuticals in which mixture experiments are important but difficult.

We can also conceive of controlled randomized experiments that use entire states as the unit of random allocation and analysis. This notion is not original: Justice Oliver Wendell Holmes reiterated the nation's interest in permitting (uncontrolled) state-wise experiments in at least one Supreme Court Decision (Breger, 1983). This is sensible where the geographical jurisdictions can be regarded as independent. In the tax expenditures arena, states might not be sufficiently independent of one another to justify an investment in controlled experiments. When individuals or small businesses are the target for exemptions, using these as the units of randomization may be reasonable. When natural corporations are the target, using states as the unit of allocation might not be sensible, but using geographic regions might be.

Randomizing states, corporations, or other entities to different treatments is not a common practice for any evaluator or sponsor of evaluations. Nonetheless, there are precedents. Neighborhoods, factories, schools and school districts, hospital wards, businesses, and police hot spots have been the units of random allocation and analysis in controlled field experiments. The programmatic contexts have been no less difficult than the tax expenditure area: fertility control, crime prevention, health, and other areas (Boruch and Foley, 1998). These macroexperiments have been complex and costly. But if unequivocal estimates of effect are of interest to the public, then political will must be joined to methodological talent to mount such experiments.

We may lack resources, much less opportunity, to run randomized controlled experiments. Moreover, alternative approaches to estimation may suffice for policy formation. Exploiting the alternatives, where appropriate, at times meets ethical standards quite apart from feasibility concerns (Federal Judicial Center, 1983). One then might employ quasi-experiments to estimate effects of tax expenditure provisions or exploit econometric models that involve much the same spirit. Each approach has similar ends despite the disciplinary differences in vernacular and method.

Chapter Four, based on work by Hanford with colleagues at the GAO, is a fine example. The problem was to establish a credible baseline or expectation of a counterfactual: what happens without an Employee Stock Ownership Plan (ESOP), using organizations as the unit of analysis. Here, as in other such settings, the creative evaluator might exploit different sources and kinds of evidence to make a fair comparison. A perspective on multiple lines of evidence was nicely laid out over ten years ago by Lipsey, Cordray, and Berger (1981).

In the GAO's study of ESOP, short time series were employed. Indicators of productivity, for example, were obtained two years before and three years after ESOP. Whether this period is sufficient is arguable. But the choice is sensible under local constraints. No theory helps us to anticipate the rate of productivity change, but at least we know now it does not happen as rapidly (if it happens at all) as advocates suggested. Furthermore, firms without an ESOP plan were identified and matched to those with ESOPs, based on industry type and size. Here, as in all quasi-experiments, whether matching variables are sufficient is unclear despite the sensibility of a match. We need to understand how non-ESOP firms perform. But we do not know if these firms are a good surrogate for the ESOP firms.

Roughly speaking, Lenjosek's analysis of Canadian tax credits in Chapter Seven also relied on multiple sources of evidence. The report is a bit less satisfying than it might have been for a reason commonly encountered in the evaluation literature: the temporal baseline, that is, the comparison time series, is not reported. We are told, for instance, that the mining tax incentives accounted for 60 percent of funding for mining exploration during 1987–91. But we are not told what the rate was for relevant precedent years, that is, 1954–86. Perhaps a period prior to 1954 is a fairer baseline, but we are told nothing about this either.

A singularly difficult issue in evaluating some expenditures programs is the need to depend on a forecast of the counterfactual condition. That is, we often lack access to a defensible comparison group, randomized or not. Rather, one must forecast how those who employ (or are eligible) for an exemption would have behaved had they not done so (or not been eligible). The approach is related to "case control studies" in the vernacular of medical clinical research. The evaluation problem is also not logically different from the idea of evaluating the "impact" of famine or war, or the Internet on this nation or world, relative to a forecast. It is hard.

None of the chapters in this volume examines deeply the problem of forecast accuracy in the tax expenditures context. This is troubling. But time here did not permit a thorough search of background reports whose authors may have considered the matter well. Certainly, direct verification of accuracy is impossible at times. As Karier put it in Chapter Six, "we cannot rerun history."

If all groups get a treatment, there is no way of verifying a forecast that presumes the treatment absent. Establishing how well forecasts are made in periods outside that covered by a tax expenditure program is nonetheless a natural option. "Backcasting," predicting the past from statistical models based on contemporary (expenditure) conditions, is another but riskier approach. Certainly understanding how well time-series forecast-based estimates of effect accord with, say, comparison group–based estimates and theory-based estimates seems important. Such work appears not to have been done or, at least, does not obviously appear in the research literature. The topic invites serious attention; it is in the nation's interest. Important research on the topic in a fine scientific, technical, and investigative tradition is reflected in recent work at the GAO and the IRS, among other federal agencies. See, for example, the U.S. General Accounting Office (1994) on cross-design synthesis in evaluating the effects of mastectomy versus lumpectomy on mortality rates of women with breast cancer, and methodological reports from the IRS's Statistics on Income Division.

What Do We Do When We Discover No Effects?

Programs in the tax expenditures arena, as in mental health, education, and criminal justice, are invented because somebody thinks the program will work.

The evaluator then evaluates, and in the best of cases, produces relatively unequivocal evidence about the program's effect.

Often, there are no discernible effects. The null hypothesis is not called this for no reason. It is sturdy in the sense that it is the ambient state. More to the point of this review, let us learn about what to do when the tax expenditure program appears not to have worked. Chapter Six is a delight on this account for industry and creativity, even if the reader might not agree with Karier's conclusions.

Recall that the Investment Tax Credit Act was enacted in 1961 and modified remarkably thereafter. The effects of the Act, including variations, could not be discerned based on arguably good evidence and analyses by Karier and his colleagues. Most important, recall that Karier asked why the effect of investment tax credits did not surface. This is an important question. Its answer depends on speculation that most evaluators, to their credit, are worried about. The approach invites attention by evaluators because understanding the plausible reasons and competing explanations for failure is at least as important as understanding the plausible reasons for success.

For example, the tax credits for corporate equipment investments have no discernible effect on purchases of the equipment despite good a priori arguments that they would. Being able to postulate ex post facto reasons why there was no effect and to generate evidence bearing on the reasons is good science. The credit changes, for instance, may be less valuable than the equipment price changes. The corporate perspective on investments of profit may have put higher value on employee wages or benefits, or on the infrastructure or the buildings, than on new equipment. These reasons are plausible. Karier's identification of them and his search for evidence that can help in judging their plausibility accord well with Campbell and Stanley's (1996) counsel on structuring how we think about such evidence.

Thinking in broader ways about this topic, in the context of studies on tax expenditures and on all other targets for evaluation, is justified. For instance, as a consequence of some good controlled tests, we are treated periodically to review essays or books on "what works." But compendiums on "what did not work" are scarce. This is also true in the medical arena, where controlled tests are run much more frequently than in the social, behavioral, and policy contexts, including education. In an attempt to reduce this gap in understanding, a new on-line *Journal of Negative Observations in the Genetic Oncology* (NOGO) has been created (Voss, 1998). We might exploit this precedent to argue for such a journal on tax expenditures, criminal justice, and employment and training, where good studies are more numerous if not ample in supply because negative effects (i.e., failure to disconfirm the conventional null hypothesis) are common in our line of work. Further, serious ex post facto explanations, despite their tentativeness, might also be published on line. There are interesting models of these published in hard copy in engineering and other disciplines, e.g., *Engineering Progress through Trouble* (Whyte, 1975).

Concluding Remarks

This issue of *New Directions* helps greatly to open a new arena for thinking about how to do evaluations well: tax expenditures. They do so directly, by defining the general topic and providing fine examples. They do so indirectly, by helping us to understand how investigations of tax expenditure systems can be framed. Reframing of the sort done in this chapter is conventional but instructive. The reports also refresh how we think about evaluation.

In the tax expenditure arena, target populations may, for example, be individuals, entities, *or* entire expenditure systems, programs, or provisions. The population chosen may be hierarchical, for instance, with states or corporations being on one level and particular stockholders, families, or individuals within the state or corporation on a second level. Here, as in other evaluation contexts, these entities may change over the course of time, and this increases the evaluators' burdens. Firms, for example, may disappear, merge, or alter their corporate state. Learning how to handle these issues better is a good topic for methodological research.

Treatment programs may be easy to identify as they are in many evaluative studies. Or they may involve treatments that are inchoate or depend on many intermediaries or brokers. Laws that govern specific tax expenditures have often changed over time, in character, scope, and intensity of their focus. Learning how to think about implementation and fidelity of program delivery then requires deep consideration. Further, time frames in tax expenditure work appear longer than in many other evaluative settings. This in turn invites the evaluator to think more in terms of archival data sets, time series, and longitudinal study of entities and individuals over decades, rather than, say, a two- to three-year period. None of these topics appears to have been subjected to intensive methodological investigation in the tax expenditures arena. They deserve better treatment.

Negotiating a choice of outcome variables to measure when a program has multiple goals is not an unusual task for evaluators. The process in the tax expenditure arena may be simple in that revenue change is ostensibly relevant. But the relevance of certain other variables can be far from clear. Behavior change in the sense of corporations' (or individuals') shifting strategy is expected of some expenditure provisions. But exactly what behavior, at what point in time, is a matter for more serious research and theory building.

Deciding how to construct the counterfactual—how to guess or estimate what would happen in the absence of the intervention—is a basic problem in evaluation. The counterfactual is the basis for comparison or estimation of a program's effects. The difficulty of the task is deep in the tax expenditures arena. Moreover, the task is more complex for the following reason. Each chapter had to rely on post-facto evaluations over a time period to estimate an effect. None of the chapters in this volume refers to any statutory tax expenditure provision that invites active experimentation.

To judge from the chapters in this volume, some evaluations of tax expenditure programs have been conscientious. But the ambiguities in evidence are also clear. In the tax expenditures arenas, the U.S. Congress and the Canadian Parliament have the opportunity to understand better the consequences of their acts. That better understanding will be achieved only if legislation on tax expenditures permits, invites, and sponsors the generation of an evaluation plan as part of the enabling legislation. Permitting active and controlled experimentation is one way to enhance scientific knowledge and public progress. Permitting the use of tax returns in research by independent scholarly researchers is another way. Permission, however, needs to be made an explicit feature of national policy.

References

Breger, M. "Randomized Social Experiments and the Law." In R. F. Boruch and J. S. Cecil (eds.), *Solutions to Legal and Ethical Problems in Applied Social Research.* New York: Academic Press, 1983, 97–144.

Boruch, R. F., and Foley, E. *Organizations and Other Entities as the Unit of Allocation and Assignment in Randomized Controlled Experiments.* Philadelphia, PA.: University of Pennsylvania, Center for Research on Evaluation and Social Policy (CRESP), 1998. (Research Report No. P-604)

Campbell, D. T., and Stanley, J. C. *Experimental and Quasi-experimental Designs.* Chicago: Rand McNally, 1996.

Corsi, J. R., and Hurley, T. L. "Attitudes Toward the Use of Telephone in Administrative Hearings." *Administrative Law Review,* 1979, *31,* 485–524.

Duncan, G. T., Jabine, T. B., and de Wolfe, V. (eds.) *Private Lives and Public Policies: Confidentiality and Accessibility of Government Statistics.* Washington, D.C.: National Academy of Sciences, 1993.

Federal Judicial Center. *Social Experimentation and the Law.* Washington, D.C.: Federal Judicial Center, United States Supreme Court, 1983.

Finn, J. D., and Achilles, C. M. "Answers and Questions about Class Size: A Statewide Experiment." *American Educational Research Journal,* 1990, *27,* 557–577.

Lipsey, M. W., Cordray, D. S., and Berger, D. E. "Evaluation of a Juvenile Diversion Program: Using Multiple Lines of Evidence." *Evaluation Review,* 1981, *5* (3), 283–306.

Perng, S. S. "Accounts Receivable Treatments Study." *New Directions for Program Evaluation,* 1985, *28,* 55–62.

Robins, P. K., Spiegelman, R. G., Weiner, S., and Bell, J. G. *A Guaranteed Annual Income: Evidence from a Social Experiment.* New York: Academic Press, 1980.

Roth, J. A., Scholz, J. R., and Witte, A. D. (eds.) *Taxpayer Compliance.* Vol. 1: *An Agenda for Research.* Philadelphia: University of Pennsylvania Press, 1989.

Schwartz, R. D., and Orleans, S. "On Legal Sanctions." *University of Chicago Law Review,* 1967, *34,* 274–300.

U.S. General Accounting Office. *Cross-Design Synthesis.* Washington, D.C.: U.S. General Accounting Office, 1994.

Voss, D. "Webwatch." *Science,* 1998, *279,* 43.

Whyte, R. R. *Engineering Progress through Trouble.* London: The Institution of Mechanical Engineers, 1975.

ROBERT F. BORUCH is University Trustee Chair professor of education at the graduate school of education and professor of statistics at the Wharton School of the University of Pennsylvania. He serves on the research and education advisory panel of the U. S. General Accounting Office, the board of directors of the American Institute of Research, and the board of trustees of the William T. Grant Foundation.

INDEX

Aaron, H. J., 2
Ability-to-pay, 14
Abt Associates Inc., 46, 47, 53, 56, 57
Achilles, C. M., 138
Adler, M., 63
Aid to Families with Dependent Children (AFDC), 30–31, 38
Analysis of covariance (ANCOVA), 70–71
Archer, Bill, 60
Attribution, 3–4: and earned income tax credit, 33
Autoregressive integrated moving average (ARIMA) analysis, 82

Balanced Budget Act of 1997, 10
Bell, J. G., 140
Berger, D. E., 141
Bird, E. J., 39
Blank, R., 30
Blasi, J. R., 72
Boruch, R. F., 7, 67
Boskin, M. J., 2
Breger, M., 140
Browning, E., 39
Budget Act of 1974, 12
Burke, E., 135
Burkhauser, R. V., 40
Butler, S. M., 78, 79

California Work Pays Demonstration Project (CWPDP), 30
Campbell, D. T., 67, 83, 143
Capital gains, 18–19
Capitalist Manifesto, The, 63
Case studies, of enterprise zones, 81–82
Committee on Ways and Means, 25, 60
Compustat Database, 110
Congressional Budget and Impoundment Control Act of 1974, 9, 12
Congressional Budget Office (CBO), 58–59
Conte, M. A., 73, 74
Cook, T. D., 83
Cordray, D. S., 141
Couch, K. A., 40
Crosse, S., 6
Cummings, J., 51

Data. *See* Tax data
Datta, L., 135
Davie, B. F., 4, 12, 136
De Long, J. B., 110, 111
Department of Finance Canada, 131
de Wolfe, V., 139
Dickert, S., 33, 36
DiPasquale, D., 51
Direct expenditures: and Low-Income Housing Tax Credit, 59–61; versus tax expenditures, 1, 16–17
Duncan, G. T., 139

Earned income tax credit (EITC), 4–5, 25–40: and Aid to Families with Dependent Children (AFDC), 30–31, 38; appropriate comparisons for, 3; compliance with, 37–39; and direct spending, 17; evaluation of, 28–39; growth of, 27–28; labor market effects of, 31–37; overview of, 25–28; participation in, 28–31; qualification requirements for, 26–27; structure of, 26–28; studies of, 30–31, 32–36, 37–39
Eissa, N., 33, 34, 35, 36, 37, 40
Employee Retirement Income Security Act of 1974, 64
Employee stock ownership plans (ESOPs), 5, 63–75: central issues in, 65–73; definition of, 64–65; history of, 63–64; impact analysis of, 66–67; lessons for future evaluations of, 73–75; performance measures for, 67–68; as tax expenditure programs, 65
Employer surveys, about enterprise zones, 83
Energy companies, and flow-through shares, 117–133
Engineering Progress through Trouble, 143
Enterprise zones (EZs), 5, 77–92: case studies of, 81–82; central issues in, 79–80; data for, 85–86; definition of, 78–79; federal program for, 90–91; findings on, 87–90; interrupted time-series analyses of, 82–83; lessons for future evaluations of, 91–92; Maryland program for, 82–90; methodological

Back Issue/Subscription Order Form

Copy or detach and send to:
Jossey-Bass Inc., Publishers, 350 Sansome Street, San Francisco CA 94104-1342
Call or fax toll free!
Phone 888-378-2537 6AM-5PM PST; Fax 800-605-2665

Back issues: Please send me the following issues at $23 each
(Important: please include series initials and issue number, such as EV90)

1. EV _____

_____

_____

$ _____ Total for single issues

$ _____ Shipping charges (for single issues *only;* subscriptions are exempt
from shipping charges): Up to $30, add $5^{50} • $30^{01}–$50, add $6^{50}
$50^{01}–$75, add $7^{50} • $75^{01}–$100, add $9 • $100^{01}–$150, add $10
Over $150, call for shipping charge

Subscriptions Please ❑ start   ❑ renew my subscription to *New Directions
for Evaluation* for the year 19___ at the following rate:

❑ Individual $65   ❑ Institutional $115
NOTE: Subscriptions are quarterly, and are for the calendar year only.
Subscriptions begin with the spring issue of the year indicated above.
For shipping outside the U.S., please add $25.

$ _____ Total single issues and subscriptions (CA, IN, NJ, NY and DC
residents, add sales tax for single issues. NY and DC residents must
include shipping charges when calculating sales tax. NY and Canadian
residents only, add sales tax for subscriptions)

❑ Payment enclosed (U.S. check or money order only)

❑ VISA, MC, AmEx, Discover Card #_____ Exp. date_____

Signature _____ Day phone _____

❑ Bill me (U.S. institutional orders only. Purchase order required)

Purchase order #_____

Name _____

Address _____

_____

_____

Phone_____ E-mail _____

For more information about Jossey-Bass Publishers, visit our Web site at:
www.josseybass.com   **PRIORITY CODE = ND1**